THE GAME OF LIFE AND HOW TO PLAY IT

Also available in the same series:

Beyond Good and Evil: The Philosophy Classic
by Friedrich Nietzsche (ISBN: 978-0-857-08848-2)

Meditations: The Philosophy Classic
by Marcus Aurelius (ISBN: 978-0-857-08846-8)

On the Origin of Species: The Science Classic
by Charles Darwin (ISBN: 978-0-857-08847-5)

Tao Te Ching: The Ancient Classic
by Lao Tzu (ISBN: 978-0-857-08311-1)

The Art of War: The Ancient Classic
by Sun Tzu (ISBN: 978-0-857-08009-7)

The Interpretation of Dreams: The Psychology Classic
by Sigmund Freud (ISBN: 978-0-857-08844-4)

The Prince: The Original Classic
by Niccolo Machiavelli (ISBN: 978-0-857-08078-3)

The Prophet: The Spiritual Classic
by Kahlil Gibran (ISBN: 978-0-857-08855-0)

The Republic: The Influential Classic
by Plato (ISBN: 978-0-857-08313-5)

The Science of Getting Rich: The Original Classic
by Wallace Wattles (ISBN: 978-0-857-08008-0)

The Wealth of Nations: The Economics Classic
by Adam Smith (ISBN: 978-0-857-08077-6)

Think and Grow Rich: The Original Classic
by Napoleon Hill (ISBN: 978-1-906-46559-9)

THE GAME OF LIFE AND HOW TO PLAY IT
The Self-Help Classic

FLORENCE SCOVEL SHINN

With an Introduction by
TOM BUTLER-BOWDON

CAPSTONE
A Wiley Brand

Registered office
John Wiley & Sons Ltd, The Atrium, Southern Gate, Chichester, West Sussex, PO19 8SQ, United Kingdom

For details of our global editorial offices, for customer services and for information about how to apply for permission to reuse the copyright material in this book please see our website at www.wiley.com.

A catalogue record for this book is available from the Library of Congress.

A catalogue record for this book is available from the British Library.

ISBN 978–0–857–08840–6 (hardback) ISBN 978–0–857–08842–0 (ebk)
ISBN 978–0–857–08837–6 (ebk)

C9780857088406_040124

Cover design: Wiley

Set in 11/15pt ITC New Baskerville by Aptara, New Delhi, India
Printed and bound by CPI Group (UK) Ltd, Croydon, CR0 4YY

CONTENTS

AN INTRODUCTION

BY TOM BUTLER-BOWDON

The Game of Life and How to Play It is not the biggest-selling self-help title of all time, nor is it the most famous. But since its appearance in 1925, Florence Scovel Shinn's short book has brought quiet inspiration and reassurance to millions. Readers find that it offers a mental release from whatever is troubling them. It provides a crucial reminder of the eternal spiritual laws that inform everything, from the flow of money to relationships to good health.

The universe works according to a perfect law of giving and receiving, Scovel Shinn said. Whatever you give out must come back to you in some form. If you love, you'll be loved. If you hate, you'll receive hate. If you lie, you'll be lied to. This for her was the central teaching of the Bible, of which she was a life-long student. She also knew it as the law of Karma. Yet it is a law that is as much a part of humanist ethics as religion. As the philosopher Immanuel Kant put it in *Critique of Practical Reason*: 'Two things fill the mind with ever new and increasing admiration and awe, the more often and steadily reflection is occupied with them: the starry heaven above me and the moral law within me.'

When we get into difficult situations, or we have some strong desire that is not being fulfilled, it is nearly always because we have forgotten universal spiritual law or have tried to thwart it. Driven by our emotions, we see the world only through the bubble of our wants and desires, irrespective of whether they are in line with the true design for our lives.

Until now, you may have conceived of life as a battle involving your will against everyone else's. But this is exhausting, and there is a path of less resistance. Scovel Shinn tried to show that the game of life makes a lot more sense when we recognize its metaphysical rules – to live in tune with the universe, not against it. By taking this path, you become a person of faith instead of fear, and live in a relaxed certainty about success.

WHO WAS SHE?

To understand Scovel Shinn and her philosophy, we need to know something of her cultural background and the spiritual tradition of which she was a part.

Florence Scovel was born in Camden, New Jersey, in 1871. Her father, Alden Cortlandt Scovel, was a lawyer. Her mother, Emily Hopkinson Scovel, came from a family that could be traced back to the early days of British settlement on America's East Coast. Emily's grandfather, Francis Hopkinson, was one of the signers of the Declaration of Independence and designed the first official American flag.

Florence attended Friends' Central School in Philadelphia, a private Quaker school. She then studied art for several years at Pennsylvania Academy of the Fine Arts. It was there that she met Everett Shinn, who was studying painting. 'Flossie' Scovel was both pretty and witty, and love blossomed. Although Everett was not a conventionally good match, it helped that he was also from a Quaker family in New Jersey.

The pair married after she graduated, and they moved to New York City. Everett worked in the theatre and Florence began to get freelance illustration jobs. As a measure of her success, in 1902 she became an associate member of the city's Society of Illustrators, at a time when it consisted almost entirely of men.

Florence Scovel Shinn, around 1902–03

The couple bought a house at 112 Waverly Place near Washington Square in Lower Manhattan. Florence spent her time illustrating for popular magazines such as *Harper's* and *Collier's*, and also worked on adult and children's books. Everett meanwhile wrote plays and formed a theatre group, the Waverly Players, with Florence sometimes acting in productions.

Everett was something of a dandy; he enjoyed the high life and would become a successful artist. He was known for his urban realist painting and was part of 'The Eight' and later the Ashcan School. Its members were known for gritty depictions of American city life, including tenement buildings, street scenes, and the life of immigrants.

Florence and Everett seemed very compatible and devoted, but according to Everett Shinn's biographer, Edith DeShazo, Florence dreaded becoming pregnant. This naturally limited their love life, and Everett began to be seen in the company of other women.

In 1912, after 14 years together, Florence filed for divorce. In court, she charged that Everett had been seen in a Broadway hotel three times with an unidentified woman, which brought tabloid headlines. She was allowed to revert to her maiden name, Scovel, and was awarded $4,800 a year in alimony – quite a lot of money in the 1920s. Everett would later lose most of his money in the Great Depression. He would have three more wives and two children.

As for Florence, a *New York Times* obituary of October 18, 1940, records her as having died at home at 1136 Fifth Avenue, 'after an illness of several weeks'. Her address, on one of New York's nicest streets and overlooking Central Park, suggests she ended her days in comfort.

What do we know of the 28 years between Florence's marriage ending in 1912, and her death at the age of 69 in 1940?

Next, let's try to reconstruct the arc of her life, and look at some of her key teachings.

UNIVERSAL ABUNDANCE

After the pain of her divorce, Florence – now in her forties – entered a period of reflection.

With her illustrator days apparently behind her, she began carving out a career as a metaphysical teacher – or what today we might call a spiritual life coach. People – mostly women – would come to her apartment and receive 'treatments'. The women were often in desperate situations involving relationships or money and needed support and solace.

In *The Game of Life*, she relates how one woman needed $3,000 by the first of the month to repay a debt, and another had to find an apartment soon or she would be on the streets. The women were asked to repeat statements such as: 'Spirit is never too late. I give thanks that I have received the money on the invisible plane and that it manifests on time.' One woman had only a day to go until a payment was due. But she took on board Florence's advice, and tried to keep calm and positive. It then happened that a cousin made a surprise visit. He asked, as he was leaving, 'By the way, how are your finances?' She was able to make her overdue payment the next day.

If you ignore prompts to be generous and cling on to your money, Scovel Shinn says, 'the same amount of money will go in an uninteresting or unhappy way'. We must always remember that the game of life is about giving and receiving. Whatever you give always comes back to you, sometimes quickly, sometimes when you least expect it. If you can constantly remind yourself that the universe is incredibly abundant, you enter the flow of universal wealth. When you insist that anything is yours alone, you cut yourself off from the flow.

SPEAK THE WORD

A woman who had hit hard times came to Florence. She was constantly on the move because of lack of funds. She had previously lived in a nice home, had beautiful things, and plenty of money. But when she was sometimes exasperated with the management of it all, she'd say, 'I'm sick and tired of things – I wish I lived in a trunk.' A couple of years later, her wish came true, and she was homeless.

The subconscious mind, Scovel Shinn says, has no sense of humour. We have to be super careful about our idle remarks, and ensure they always conform to a positive view of life. Even if at present we have little money or love in our life, we should bless what little we have. If we're thankful that there is so much abundance and love in the world, it's more likely that we'll develop a relaxed certainty that more will flow to us. If we focus on what we lack, that will create its manifestation in reality.

Why is Scovel Shinn so focused on the spoken word? There is a Quaker saying: 'When you pray, move your feet'. This means that although universal law or God is all powerful, we are at the same time co-creators of the universe. We have to make the first move, she says, whether that means a statement, a desire, or something imagined.

The people who came to see Florence would ask her to 'speak the word'. She would give them some affirmation for their particular situation which they had to go away and state many times a day, sometimes over a period of months. If they persisted, they often had miraculous results. The reason, she would explain, is that the positive words create an aura of protection around the person who speaks them. When we eliminate the negativity within ourselves, we can't be influenced by the negativity in others. By blessing your enemy, he or she is robbed of their ammunition.

THE DIVINE DESIGN

Sometimes, we get a mental flash of what we could achieve, or the person we could be. It comes across as too good to be true, so we dismiss it from our minds. In fact, Scovel Shinn says, we've actually received a snapshot of our 'divine design' from the universe – a unique promise that only we can fulfil. Plato called it the 'perfect pattern', and it's our job to see it realized. If you don't yet know what your life is about, she told her clients, ask for a sign or a message. Don't be scared that it won't be what you want, as it will invariably fulfil your deepest longing.

Part of your divine design may be a relationship. Scovel Shinn tells how a woman came to her who was desperately in love with a man who seemed to want nothing to do with her. She wanted Florence to 'speak the word' so that the man would come around. But Florence refused. She instead invoked the power of 'divine selection': if this man was right for the woman according to universal law, he would come to her. If he wasn't, he'd fall out of the picture.

What happened? Not long after, the woman quickly fell in love with another man, and wondered what she'd ever seen in the first one. The message: let universal intelligence, or God, or the power within you (call it what you like, but it must be beyond the normal conscious mind) decide if something accords with your divine design. The answer you get will be infallible.

THE UNIVERSE IS POWERED BY FAITH

Life seems to be so solid that it's tempting to only look at 'the facts' in the here and now. Yet much of our reality has come into being through things that people once only imagined. The game of life seems to be won by those who choose faith over fear. As Scovel Shinn puts it, 'Man must prepare for the thing he has asked for, *when there isn't the slightest sign of it in sight.*' It's precisely at this point that we need to be assured, giving thanks that what we've imagined has already been received. Looking back on your life so far and what you've achieved, it's more likely that you thought too small, not too big. Be like Jesus, the Buddha, and all the other spiritual giants, she says, who understood that clear vision and faith make light work of the apparently heavy world of matter.

Fear is 'sin' – it goes against nature, whereas faith is real, solid, and is the thing that Infinite Intelligence or God requires from us in return for delivering our wishes. Faith is what links you to the universe; it expands your cosmic footprint, while fear can only shrink you.

NEW THOUGHT, NEW LIFE

Many of Florence's ideas came from her involvement in the religious organization known as Unity.

Unity today describes itself as 'A worldwide Spiritual Movement dedicated to helping people discover and express their divine potential'. Although its teachings are mainly drawn from the Old and New Testaments, it holds that spiritual truth is too vast to be contained by any one religion or philosophy. It's a very practical, non-dogmatic form of Christianity whose focus is the application of universal moral law or 'infinite intelligence' to everyday life situations. What also sets it apart from mainstream Christian churches is the leading role that women have played in the organization.

Unity was begun by Kansas City couple Charles and Myrtle Fillmore in 1889. Myrtle endured chronic tuberculosis but believed she had been cured by the power of prayer and spiritual healing. The Fillmores were strongly influenced by philosopher Ralph Waldo Emerson, Christian Science founder Mary Baker Eddy, and New Thought thinker Emma Curtis Hopkins. One of the organization's first publications was Emilie Cady's *Lessons In Truth* (1896), the bestselling bible of 'practical Christianity'.

Unity was part of the wider New Thought movement, whose philosophers included Prentice Mulford and William Walker Atkinson. Its ideas about positive thinking, the law of attraction, mental healing, and creative visualization would come to have a huge impact on mainstream culture through the self-help literature. Motivational classics such as Napoleon Hill's *Think and Grow Rich* are soaked in New Thought ideas, as are many contemporary spiritual bestsellers such as *The Secret*.

Florence would have read the key New Thought books. Her spiritual advisor was Richard Lynch, who had studied under the Fillmores, and who had founded the Manhattan branch of Unity that she attended. Although Florence never became a Unity minister, she spoke each week at its Manhattan services and also gave public lectures at venues such as Steinway Hall. A biographical note at the back of the 1938 edition of *The Game of Life* says:

She addresses the public at Unity-New York, 33 West 39th Street, every Sunday morning at 11 o'clock, Thursday evening at 8:15 and Friday afternoon at 2:30, giving treatments and interviews after the meetings, or by appointment.

As a divorced single woman with a Quaker background, it is easy to understand how Florence was attracted to this open-minded church and its powerful teachings. As she began her work as a spiritual coach for people in need, probably in the mid to late 1910s, Unity's metaphysical system fed her constant inspiration. At some point it would have occurred to her that she could make New Thought metaphysics come alive for a broader audience by expressing it through the stories of her clients.

She decided to write a book, but Florence's attempts to find a publisher for *The Game of Life and How to Play It* failed. Undaunted, she published it herself, and sold it through the bookshop of the Unity church. The brilliant title, its intriguing and inspiring content, plus public awareness of Florence through her speaking, made the book sell. That in turn led more people to seek her out in private practice.

Three years later, she followed it with *Your Word Is Your Wand* (1928). There was a long break in publication, then just before her death came *The Secret Door to Success* (1940), with more stories from her practice. We include it as a bonus in this Capstone Classics edition. Florence's followers also put together some of her notes after her death, publishing *The Power of the Spoken Word* in 1945.

LEGACY

The New Thought writer Emmet Fox, who was minister at New York's Divine Science church, gave this eulogy for Florence:

> One secret of Shinn's success was that she was always herself … colloquial, informal, friendly, and humorous. She never sought to be literary, conventional, or impressive. For this reason she appealed to thousands who would not have taken the spiritual message through more conservative and dignified forms, or have been willing to read … at least in the beginning … the standard metaphysical books.

Florence's down-to-earth writing style, her spiritual knowledge, and her deep compassion for her clients and readers created something timeless. She may not have expected that her books, with their old-fashioned turns of phrase and often quaint anecdotes from 1920s and 1930s America, would still be read today. The times may change, but people's fundamental concerns do not. Whatever the era, we seek to love and be loved, we desire good health, and we want material security for ourselves and our children.

At a low point in her life, author Louise Hay (*You Can Heal Your Life*) discovered Florence's writings at a Christian Science Reading Room in New York. They helped turn her life around. The motivational writer Norman Vincent Peale (*The Power of Positive Thinking*) knew and enjoyed her work, as did Yolanda King, daughter of Martin Luther King Jr.

Almost a century after the publication of *The Game of Life and How to Play It*, Florence's words still have the ability to move and inspire us. Having taught us how, we too have the power to 'speak the word' and live the life that was designed for us.

ABOUT TOM BUTLER-BOWDON

Tom Butler-Bowdon is the author of the bestselling 50 Classics series, which brings the ideas of important books to a wider audience. Titles include *50 Philosophy Classics*, *50 Psychology Classics*, *50 Politics Classics*, *50 Self-Help Classics* and *50 Economics Classics*.

As series editor for the Capstone Classics series, Tom has written Introductions to Plato's *The Republic*, Machiavelli's *The Prince*, Adam Smith's *The Wealth of Nations*, Sun Tzu's *The Art of War*, Lao Tzu's *Tao Te Ching*, and Napoleon Hill's *Think and Grow Rich*.

Tom is a graduate of the London School of Economics and the University of Sydney.

www.Butler-Bowdon.com

THE GAME OF LIFE
AND HOW TO PLAY IT

CONTENTS

I

THE GAME

Most people consider life a battle, but it is not a battle, it is a game.

It is a game, however, which cannot be played successfully without the knowledge of spiritual law, and the Old and the New Testaments give the rules of the game with wonderful clearness. Jesus Christ taught that it was a great game of *Giving and Receiving.*

"Whatsoever a man soweth that shall he also reap." This means that whatever man sends out in word or deed, will return to him; what he gives, he will receive.

If he gives hate, he will receive hate; if he gives love, he will receive love; if he gives criticism, he will receive criticism; if he lies he will be lied to; if he cheats he will be cheated. We are taught also, that the imaging faculty plays a leading part in the game of life.

"Keep thy heart (or imagination) with all diligence, for out of it are the issues of life." (Prov. 4:23.)

This means that what man images, sooner or later externalizes in his affairs. I know of a man who feared a certain disease. It was a very rare disease and difficult to get, but he pictured it continually and read about it until it manifested in his body, and he died, the victim of distorted imagination.

So we see, to play successfully the game of life, we must train the imaging faculty. A person with an imaging faculty trained to image only good, brings into his life "every righteous desire of his heart"—health, wealth, love, friends, perfect self-expression, his highest ideals.

The imagination has been called, "*The Scissors of The Mind*," and it is ever cutting, cutting, day by day, the pictures man sees there, and sooner or later he meets his own creations in his outer world. To train the imagination successfully, man must understand the workings of his mind. The Greeks said: "Know Thyself."

There are three departments of the mind, the *subconscious, conscious and superconscious*. The subconscious, is simply power, without direction. It is like steam or electricity, and it does what it is directed to do; it has no power of induction.

Whatever man feels deeply or images clearly, is impressed upon the subconscious mind, and carried out in minutest detail.

For example: a woman I know, when a child, always "made believe" she was a widow. She "dressed up" in black clothes and wore a long black veil, and people thought she was very clever and amusing. She grew up and married a man with whom she was deeply in love. In a short time he died and she wore black and a sweeping veil for many years. The picture of herself as a widow was impressed upon the subconscious mind, and in due time worked itself out, regardless of the havoc created.

The conscious mind has been called mortal or carnal mind.

CHAPTER I

It is the human mind and sees life as it *appears to be*. It sees death, disaster, sickness, poverty and limitation of every kind, and it impresses the subconscious.

The *superconscious* mind is the God Mind within each man, and is the realm of perfect ideas.

In it, is the "*perfect pattern*" spoken of by Plato, *The Divine Design;* for there is a *Divine Design* for each person.

"There is a place that you are to fill and no one else can fill, something you are to do, which no one else can do."

There is a perfect picture of this in the *super-conscious mind.* It usually flashes across the conscious as an unattainable ideal—"something too good to be true."

In reality it is man's true destiny (or destination) flashed to him from the Infinite Intelligence which is *within himself.*

Many people, however, are in ignorance of their true destinies and are striving for things and situations which do not belong to them, and would only bring failure and dissatisfaction if attained.

For example: A woman came to me and asked me to "speak the word" that she would marry a certain man with whom she was very much in love. (She called him A. B.)

I replied that this would be a violation of spiritual law, but that I would speak the word for the right man, the "divine selection," the man who belonged to her by divine right.

I added, "If A. B. is the right man you can't lose him, and if he isn't, you will receive his equivalent." She saw A. B. frequently but no headway was made in their friendship. One evening she called, and said, "Do you know, for the last week, A. B. hasn't seemed so wonderful to me." I replied, "Maybe he is not the divine selection—another man may be the right one." Soon after that, she met another man who fell in love with her at once, and who said she was his ideal. In fact, he said all the things that she had always wished A. B. would say to her.

She remarked, "It was quite uncanny."

She soon returned his love, and lost all interest in A. B.

This shows the law of substitution. A right idea was substituted for a wrong one, therefore there was no loss or sacrifice involved.

Jesus Christ said, "Seek ye first the Kingdom of God and his righteousness; and all these things shall be added unto you," and he said the Kingdom *was within man.*

The Kingdom is the realm of *right ideas*, or the divine pattern.

Jesus Christ taught that man's words played a leading part in the game of life. "By your words ye are justified and by your words ye are condemned."

Many people have brought disaster into their lives through idle words.

For example: A woman once asked me why her life was now one of poverty of limitation. Formerly she had a home, was surrounded by beautiful things and had plenty of money. We found she had often tired of the management of her home, and had said repeatedly, "I'm sick and tired of things—I wish I lived in a trunk," and she added: "Today I am living in that trunk." She had spoken herself into a trunk. The subconscious mind has no sense of humor and people often joke themselves into unhappy experiences.

CHAPTER I

For example: A woman who had a great deal of money, joked continually about "getting ready for the poorhouse."

In a few years she was almost destitute, having impressed the subconscious mind with a picture of lack and limitation.

Fortunately the law works both ways, and a situation of lack may be changed to one of plenty.

For example: A woman came to me one hot summer's day for a "treatment" for prosperity. She was worn out, dejected and discouraged. She said she possessed just eight dollars in the world. I said, "Good, we'll bless the eight dollars and multiply them as Jesus Christ multiplied the loaves and the fishes," for He taught that every man had the power to bless and to multiply, to heal and to prosper.

She said, "What shall I do next?"

I replied, "Follow intuition. Have you a 'hunch' to do anything, or to go anywhere?" Intuition means, intuition, or to be taught from within. It is man's unerring guide, and I will deal more fully with its laws in a following chapter.

The woman replied: "I don't know—I seem to have a 'hunch' to go home; I've just enough money for carfare." Her home was in a distant city and was one of lack and limitation, and the reasoning mind (or intellect) would have said: "Stay in New York and get work and make some money." I replied, "Then go home—never violate a hunch." I spoke the following words for her: "*Infinite Spirit open the way for great abundance for— —. She is an irresistible magnet for all that belongs to her by divine right.*" I told her to repeat it continually also. She left for home immediately. In calling on a woman one day, she linked up with an old friend of her family.

Through this friend, she received thousands of dollars in a most miraculous way. She has said to me often, "Tell people about the woman who came to you with eight dollars and a hunch."

There is always *plenty on man's pathway;* but it can only be *brought into manifestation* through desire, faith or the spoken word. Jesus Christ brought out clearly that man must make the *first move.*

"*Ask,* and it shall be given you, seek, and ye shall find, knock, and it shall be opened unto you." (Mat. 7:7.)

In the Scriptures we read:

"Concerning the works of my hands, command ye me."

Infinite Intelligence, God, is ever ready to carry out man's smallest or greatest demands.

Every desire, uttered or unexpressed, is a demand. We are often startled by having a wish suddenly fulfilled.

For example: One Easter, having seen many beautiful rose-trees in the florists' windows, I wished I would receive one, and for an instant saw it mentally being carried in the door.

Easter came, and with it a beautiful rose-tree. I thanked my friend the following day, and told her it was just what I had wanted.

She replied, "I didn't send you a rose-tree, I sent you lilies!"

The man had mixed the order, and sent me a rose-tree simply because I had started the law in action, and *I had to have a rose-tree.*

Nothing stands between man and his highest ideals and every desire of his heart, but doubt and fear. When man can "wish without worrying," every desire will be instantly fulfilled.

CHAPTER I

I will explain more fully in a following chapter the scientific reason for this and how fear must be erased from the consciousness. It is man's only enemy—fear of lack, fear of failure, fear of sickness, fear of loss and a feeling of *insecurity on some plane.* Jesus Christ said: "Why are ye fearful, oh ye of little faith?" (Mat. 8:26.) So we can see we must substitute faith for fear, for fear is only inverted faith; it is faith in evil instead of good.

The object of the game of life is to see clearly one's good and to obliterate all mental pictures of evil. This must be done by impressing the subconscious mind with a realization of good. A very brilliant man, who has attained great success, told me he had suddenly erased all fear from his consciousness by reading a sign which hung in a room. He saw printed, in large letters this statement—"*Why worry, it will probably never happen.*" These words were stamped indelibly upon his subconscious mind, and he has now a firm conviction that only good can come into his life, therefore only *good can manifest.*

In the following chapter I will deal with the different methods of impressing the subconscious mind. It is man's faithful servant but one must be careful to give it the right orders. Man has ever a silent listener at his side—his subconscious mind.

Every thought, every word is impressed upon it and carried out in amazing detail. It is like a singer making a record on the sensitive disc of the phonographic plate. Every note and tone of the singer's voice is registered. If he coughs or hesitates, it is registered also. So let us break all the old bad records in the subconscious mind, the records of our lives which we do not wish to keep, and make new and beautiful ones.

Speak these words aloud, with power and conviction: "I now smash and demolish (by my spoken word) every untrue record in my subconscious mind. They shall return to the dust-heap of their native nothingness, for they came from my own vain imaginings. I now make my perfect records through the Christ within—The records of *Health, Wealth, Love and perfect self-Expression.*" This is the square of life, *The Game completed.*

In the following chapters, I will show how man can *change his conditions by changing his words.* Any man who does not know the power of the word, is behind the times.

"Death and Life are in the power of the tongue."

(Prov. 18:21.)

THE LAW OF PROSPERITY

"Yea, the Almighty shall be thy defense and thou shalt have plenty of silver."

One of the greatest messages given to the race through the scriptures is that God is man's supply and that man can release, *through his spoken word,* all that belongs to him by divine right. He must, however, have *perfect faith in his spoken word.*

Isaiah said, "My word shall not return unto me void, but shall accomplish that where unto it is sent." We know now, that words and thoughts are a tremendous vibratory force, ever moulding man's body and affairs.

A woman came to me in great distress and said she was to be sued on the fifteenth of the month for three thousand dollars. She knew no way of getting the money and was in despair.

I told her God was her supply, and *that there is a supply for every demand.*

So I spoke the word! I gave thanks that the woman would receive three thousand dollars at the right time in the right way. I told her she must have perfect faith, and act her *perfect faith.* The fifteenth came but no money had materialized.

She called me on the 'phone and asked what she was to do.

I replied, "It is Saturday, so they won't sue you today. Your part is to act rich, thereby showing perfect faith that you will receive it by Monday." She asked me to lunch with her to keep up her courage. When I joined her at a restaurant, I said, "This is no time to economize. Order an expensive luncheon, act as if you have already received the three thousand dollars."

"All things whatsoever ye ask in prayer, *believing*, ye shall receive." "You must act as if you had *already received*." The next morning she called me on the 'phone and asked me to stay with her during the day. I said "No, you are divinely protected and God is never too late."

In the evening she 'phoned again, greatly excited and said, "My dear, a miracle has happened! I was sitting in my room this morning, when the doorbell rang. I said to the maid: 'Don't let anyone in.' The maid however, looked out the window and said, 'It's your cousin with the long white beard.'

So I said, 'Call him back. I would like to see him.' He was just turning the corner, when he heard the maid's voice, and *he came back.*

He talked for about an hour, and just as he was leaving he said, 'Oh, by the way, how are finances?'

I told him I needed the money, and he said, 'Why, my dear, I will give you three thousand dollars the first of the month.'

I didn't like to tell him I was going to be sued. What shall I do? I won't *receive it till* the first of the month, and I must have it tomorrow." I said, "I'll keep on 'treating.'"

I said, "Spirit is never too late. I give thanks she has received the money on the invisible plane and that it manifests on time." The next morning her cousin called her up and said, "Come to my office this morning and I will give you the money." That afternoon, she had three thousand dollars to her credit in the bank, and wrote checks as rapidly as her excitement would permit.

If one asks for success and prepares for failure, he will get the situation he has prepared for. For example: A man came to me asking me to speak the word that a certain debt would be wiped out.

I found he spent his time planning what he would say to the man when he did not pay his bill, thereby neutralizing my words. He should have seen himself paying the debt.

We have a wonderful illustration of this in the bible, relating to the three kings who were in the desert, without water for their men and horses. They consulted the prophet Elisha, who gave them this astonishing message:

"Thus saith the Lord—Ye shall not see wind, neither shall ye see rain, yet make this valley full of ditches."

Man must prepare for the thing he has asked for, *when there isn't the slightest sign of it in sight.*

For example: A woman found it necessary to look for an apartment during the year when there was a great shortage of apartments in New York. It was considered almost an impossibility, and her friends were sorry for her and said, "Isn't it too bad, you'll have to store your furniture and live in a hotel." She replied, "*You needn't feel sorry for me, I'm a superman, and I'll get an apartment.*"

She spoke the words: "*Infinite Spirit, open the way for the right apartment.*" She knew there was a supply for every demand, and that she was "unconditioned," working on the spiritual plane, and that "one with God is a majority."

She had contemplated buying new blankets, when "the tempter," the adverse thought or reasoning mind, suggested, "Don't buy the blankets, perhaps, after all, you won't get an apartment and you will have no use for them." She promptly replied (to herself): "I'll dig my ditches by buying the blankets!" So she prepared for the apartment—acted as though she already had it.

She found one in a miraculous way, and it was given to her although there were over *two hundred other applicants.*

The blankets showed active faith.

It is needless to say that the ditches dug by the three kings in the desert were filled to over-flowing. (Read, II Kings.)

Getting into the spiritual swing of things is no easy matter for the average person. The adverse thoughts of doubt and fear surge from the subconscious. They are the "army of the aliens" which must be put to flight. This explains why it is so often, "darkest before the dawn."

A big demonstration is usually preceded by tormenting thoughts.

Having made a statement of high spiritual truth one challenges the old beliefs in the subconscious, and "error is exposed" to be put out.

This is the time when one must make his affirmations of truth repeatedly, and rejoice and give thanks that he has already received. "Before ye call I shall answer." This means that "every good and perfect gift" is already man's awaiting his recognition.

Man can only receive what he sees himself receiving.

The children of Israel were told that they could have all the land they could see. This is true of every man. He has

CHAPTER II

only the land within his own mental vision. Every great work, every big accomplishment, has been brought into manifestation through holding to the vision, and often just before the big achievement, comes apparent failure and discouragement.

The children of Israel when they reached the "Promised Land," were afraid to go in, for they said it was filled with giants who made them feel like grasshoppers. "And there we saw the giants and we were in our own sight as grass-hoppers." This is almost every man's experience.

However, the one who knows spiritual law, is undisturbed by appearance, and rejoices while he is "yet in captivity." That is, he holds to his vision and gives thanks that the end is accomplished, he has received.

Jesus Christ gave a wonderful example of this. He said to his disciples: "Say not ye, there are yet four months and then cometh the harvest? Behold, I say unto you, lift up your eyes and look on the fields; for they are ripe already to harvest." His clear vision pierced the "world of matter" and he saw clearly the fourth dimensional world, things as they really are, perfect and complete in Divine Mind.

So man must ever hold the vision of his journey's end and demand the manifestation of that which he has already received. It maybe his perfect health, love, supply, self-expression, home or friends.

They are all finished and perfect ideas registered in Divine Mind (man's own superconscious mind) and must come through him, not to him. For example: A man came to me asking for treatments for success. It was imperative that he raise, within a certain time, fifty-thousand dollars for his business. The time limit was almost up, when he came to me in despair.

17

No one wanted to invest in his enterprise, and the bank had flatly refused a loan. I replied: "I suppose you lost your temper while at the bank, therefore your power. You can control any situation if you first control yourself." "Go back to the bank," I added, "and I will treat." My treatment was: "You are identified in love with the spirit of everyone connected with the bank. Let the divine idea come out of this situation." He replied, "Woman, you are talking about an impossibility. Tomorrow is Saturday; the bank closes at twelve, and my train won't get me there until ten, and the time limit is up tomorrow, and anyway they won't do it. It's too late." I replied, "God doesn't need any time and is never too late. With Him all things are possible." I added, "I don't know anything about business, but I know all about God." He replied: "It all sounds fine when I sit here listening to you, but when I go out it's terrible." He lived in a distant city, and I did not hear from him for a week, then came a letter. It read: "You were right. I raised the money, and will never again doubt the truth of all that you told me."

I saw him a few weeks later, and I said, "What happened? You evidently had plenty of time, after all." He replied "My train was late, and I got there just fifteen minutes to twelve. I walked into the bank quietly and said, 'I have come for the loan,' and they gave it to me without a question."

It was the last fifteen minutes of the time allotted to him, and Infinite Spirit was not too late. In this instance the man could never have demonstrated alone. He needed someone to help him hold to the vision. This is what one man can do for another.

Jesus Christ knew the truth of this when he said: "If two of you shall agree on earth as touching anything that they shall ask, it shall be done for them of my Father which is in heaven." One gets too close to his own affairs and becomes doubtful and fearful.

The friend or "healer" sees clearly the success, health, or prosperity, and never wavers, because he is not close to the situation.

It is much easier to "demonstrate" for someone else than for one's self, so a person should not hesitate to ask for help, if he feels himself wavering.

A keen observer of life once said, "no man can fail, if some one person sees him successful." Such is the power of the vision, and many a great man has owed his success to a wife, or sister, or a friend who "believed in him" and held without wavering to the perfect pattern!

III

THE POWER OF THE WORD

"By thy words thou shalt be justified, and by thy words thou shalt be condemned."

A person knowing the power of the word, becomes very careful of his conversation. He has only to watch the reaction of his words to know that they do "not return void." Through his spoken word, man is continually making laws for himself.

I knew a man who said, "I always miss a car. It invariably pulls out just as I arrive."

His daughter said: "I always catch a car. It's sure to come just as I get there." This occurred for years. Each had made a separate law for himself, one of failure, one of success. This is the psychology of superstitions.

The horse-shoe or rabbit's foot contains no power, but man's spoken word and belief that it will bring him good luck creates expectancy in the subconscious mind, and attracts a "lucky situation." I find however, this will not "work" when man has advanced spiritually and knows a higher law. One cannot turn back, and must put away "graven images." For example: Two men in my class had had great success in business for several months, when suddenly everything "went to smash." We tried to analyze the situation, and I found, instead of making

their affirmations and looking to God for success and prosperity, they had each bought a "lucky monkey." I said: "Oh
I see, you have been trusting in the lucky monkeys instead
of God." "Put away the lucky monkeys and call on the law of
forgiveness," for man has power to forgive or neutralize his
mistakes.

They decided to throw the lucky monkeys down a coalhole,
and all went well again. This does not mean, however, that one
should throw away every "lucky" ornament or horse-shoe about
the house, but he must recognize that the power back of it is
the one and only power, God, and that the object simply gives
him a feeling of expectancy.

I was with a friend, one day, who was in deep despair. In
crossing the street, she picked up a horseshoe. Immediately,
she was filled with joy and hope. She said God had sent her
the horseshoe in order to keep up her courage.

It was indeed, at that moment, about the only thing that
could have registered in her consciousness. Her hope became
faith, and she ultimately made a wonderful demonstration. I
wish to make the point clear that the men previously mentioned were depending on the monkeys, alone, while this
woman recognized the power back of the horseshoe.

I know, in my own case, it took a long while to get out of
a belief that a certain thing brought disappointment. If the
thing happened, disappointment invariably followed. I found
the only way I could make a change in the subconscious, was
by asserting, "There are not two powers, there is only one
power, God, therefore, there are no disappointments, and this
thing means a happy surprise." I noticed a change at once, and
happy surprises commenced coming my way.

I have a friend who said nothing could induce her to walk under a ladder. I said, "If you are afraid, you are giving in to a belief in two powers, Good and Evil, instead of one. As God is absolute, there can be no opposing power, unless man makes the false of evil for himself. To show you believe in only One Power, God, and that there is no power or reality in evil, walk under the next ladder you see." Soon after, she went to her bank. She wished to open her box in the safety-deposit vault, and there stood a ladder on her pathway. It was impossible to reach the box without passing under the ladder. She quailed with fear and turned back. She could not face the lion on her pathway. However, when she reached the street, my words rang in her ears and she decided to return and walk under it. It was a big moment in her life, for ladders had held her in bondage for years. She retraced her steps to the vault, and the ladder was no longer there! This so often happens! If one is willing to do a thing he is afraid to do, he does not have to.

It is the law of nonresistance, which is so little understood.

Someone has said that courage contains genius and magic. Face a situation fearlessly, and there is no situation to face; it falls away of its own weight.

The explanation is, that fear attracted the ladder on the woman's pathway, and fearlessness removed it.

Thus the invisible forces are ever working for man who is always "pulling the strings" himself, though he does not know it. Owing to the vibratory power of words, whatever man voices, he begins to attract. People who continually speak of disease, invariably attract it.

After man knows the truth, he cannot be too careful of his words. For example: I have a friend who often says on the 'phone, "Do come to see me and have a fine old-fashioned chat." This "old-fashioned chat" means an hour of about five hundred to a thousand destructive words, the principal topics being loss, lack, failure and sickness.

I reply: "No, I thank you, I've had enough old-fashioned chats in my life, they are too expensive, but I will be glad to have a new-fashioned chat, and talk about what we want, not what we don't want." There is an old saying that man only dares use his words for three purposes, to "heal, bless or prosper." What man says of others will be said of him, and what he wishes for another, he is wishing for himself.

"Curses, like chickens, come home to roost."

If a man wishes someone "bad luck," he is sure to attract bad luck himself. If he wishes to aid someone to success, he is wishing and aiding himself to success.

The body may be renewed and transformed through the spoken word and clear vision, and disease be completely wiped out of the consciousness. The metaphysician knows that all disease has a mental correspondence, and in order to heal the body one must first "heal the soul."

The soul is the subconscious mind, and it must be "saved" from wrong thinking.

In the twenty-third psalm, we read: "He restoreth my soul." This means that the subconscious mind or soul, must be restored with the right ideas, and the "mystical marriage" is the marriage of the soul and the spirit, or the subconscious and superconscious mind. They must be one. When the subconscious is flooded with the perfect ideas of the superconscious, God and man are one. "I and the Father are one." That is, he is one with the realm of perfect ideas; he is the man made in God's likeness and image (imagination) and is given power and dominion over all created things, his mind, body and affairs.

It is safe to say that all sickness and unhappiness come from the violation of the law of love. A new commandment I give unto you, "Love one another," and in the Game of Life, love or good-will takes every trick.

For example: A woman I know, had, for years an appearance of a terrible skin disease. The doctors told her it was incurable, and she was in despair. She was on the stage, and she feared she would soon have to give up her profession, and she had no other means of support. She, however, procured a good engagement, and on the opening night, made a great "hit." She received flattering notices from the critics, and was joyful and elated. The next day she received a notice of dismissal. A man in the cast had been jealous of her success and had caused her to be sent away. She felt hatred and resentment taking complete possession of her, and she cried out, "Oh God don't let me hate that man." That night she worked for hours "in the silence."

She said, "I soon came into a very deep silence. I seemed to be at peace with myself, with the man, and with the whole world. I continued this for two following nights, and on the third day I found I was healed completely of the skin disease!" In asking for love, or good will, she had fulfilled the law, ("for love is the fulfilling of the law") and the disease (which came from subconscious resentment) was wiped out.

Continual criticism produces rheumatism, as critical, inharmonious thoughts cause unnatural deposits in the blood, which settle in the joints.

False growths are caused by jealousy, hatred, unforgiveness, fear, etc. Every disease is caused by a mind not at ease. I
said once, in my class, "There is no use asking anyone 'What's
the matter with you?' we might just as well say, 'Who's the matter with you?'" Unforgiveness is the most prolific cause of disease. It will harden arteries or liver, and affect the eye-sight. In
its train are endless ills.

I called on a woman, one day, who said she was ill from
having eaten a poisoned oyster. I replied, "Oh, no, the oyster
was harmless, you poisoned the oyster. What's the matter with
you?" She answered, "Oh about nineteen people." She had
quarrelled with nineteen people and had become so inharmonious that she attracted the wrong oyster.

Any inharmony on the external, indicates there is mental
inharmony. "As the within, so the without."

Man's only enemies are within himself. "And a man's foes
shall be they of his own household." Personality is one of the
last enemies to be overcome, as this planet is taking its initiation in love. It was Christ's message—"Peace on Earth, good
will towards man." The enlightened man, therefore, endeavors
to perfect himself upon his neighbor. His work is with himself,
to send out goodwill and blessings to every man, and the marvelous thing is, that if one blesses a man he has no power to
harm him.

For example: A man came to me asking to "treat" for success in business. He was selling machinery, and a rival appeared
on the scene with what he proclaimed, was a better machine,
and my friend feared defeat. I said, "First of all, we must wipe
out all fear, and know that God protects your interests, and
that the divine idea must come out of the situation. That is,

the right machine will be sold, by the right man, to the right man." And I added, "Don't hold one critical thought towards that man. Bless him all day, and be willing not to sell your machine, if it isn't the divine idea." So he went to the meeting, fearless and nonresistant, and blessing the other man. He said the outcome was very remarkable. The other man's machine refused to work, and he sold his without the slightest difficulty. "But I say unto you, love your enemies, bless them that curse you, do good to them that hate you, and pray for them which spitefully use you and persecute you."

Good-will produces a great aura of protection about the one who sends it, and "No weapon that is formed against him shall prosper." In other words, love and good-will destroy the enemies within one's self, therefore, one has no enemies on the external!

"There is peace on earth for him who sends goodwill to man!"

THE LAW OF NONRESISTANCE

"Resist not evil. Be not overcome of evil, but overcome evil with good."

Nothing on earth can resist an absolutely nonresistant person.

The Chinese say that water is the most powerful element, because it is perfectly nonresistant. It can wear away a rock, and sweep all before it.

Jesus Christ said, "Resist not evil," for He knew in reality, there is no evil, therefore nothing to resist. Evil has come of man's "vain imagination," or a belief in two powers, good and evil.

There is an old legend, that Adam and Eve ate of "Maya the Tree of Illusion," and saw two powers instead of one power, God.

Therefore, evil is a false law man has made for himself, through psychoma or soul sleep. Soul sleep means, that man's soul has been hypnotized by the race belief (of sin, sickness and death, etc.) which is carnal or mortal thought, and his affairs have out-pictured his illusions.

We have read in a preceding chapter, that man's soul is his subconscious mind, and whatever he feels deeply, good or bad, is outpictured by that faithful servant. His body and affairs show forth what he has been picturing. The sick man has pictured sickness, the poor man, poverty, the rich man, wealth.

People often say, "why does a little child attract illness, when it is too young even to know what it means?"

I answer that children are sensitive and receptive to the thoughts of others about them, and often outpicture the fears of their parents.

I heard a metaphysician once say, "If you do not run your subconscious mind yourself, someone else will run it for you."

Mothers often, unconsciously, attract illness and disaster to their children, by continually holding them in thoughts of fear, and watching for symptoms.

For example: A friend asked a woman if her little girl had had the measles. She replied promptly, "not yet!" This implied that she was expecting the illness, and, therefore, preparing the way for what she did not want for herself and child.

However, the man who is centered and established in right thinking, the man who sends out only good-will to his fellow-man, and who is without fear, cannot be *touched or influenced by the negative thoughts of others*. In fact, he could then receive only good thoughts, as he himself, sends forth only good thoughts.

Resistance is Hell, for it places man in a "state of torment."

A metaphysician once gave me a wonderful recipe for taking every trick in the game of life, it is the acme of nonresistance. He gave it in this way; "At one time in my life, I baptized children, and of course, they had many names. Now I no longer baptize children, but I baptize events, but *I give every event the same name*. If I have a failure I baptize it success, in the name of the Father, and of the Son, and of the Holy Ghost!"

CHAPTER IV

In this, we see the great law of transmutation, founded on nonresistance. Through his spoken word, every failure was transmuted into success.

For example: A woman who required money, and who knew the spiritual law of opulence, was thrown continually in a business-way, with a man who made her feel very poor. He talked lack and limitation and she commenced to catch his poverty thoughts, so she disliked him, and blamed him for her failure. She knew in order to demonstrate her supply, she must first feel that she had received—*a feeling of opulence must precede its manifestation.*

It dawned upon her, one day, that she was resisting the situation, and seeing two powers instead of one. So she blessed the man and baptized the situation "Success"! She affirmed, "As there is only one power, God, this man is here for my good and my prosperity" (just what he did not seem to be there for). Soon after that she met, *through this man,* a woman who gave her for a service rendered, several thousand dollars, and the man moved to a distant city, and faded harmoniously from her life. Make the statement, "Every man is a golden link in the chain of my good," for all men are God in manifestation, *awaiting the opportunity given by man, himself, to serve the divine plan of his life.*

"Bless your enemy, and you rob him of his ammunition." His arrows will be transmuted into blessings.

This law is true of nations as well as individuals. Bless a nation, send love and good-will to every inhabitant, and it is robbed of its power to harm.

Man can only get the right idea of nonresistance, through spiritual understanding. My students have often said: "I don't want to be a door-mat." I reply "when you use nonresistance with wisdom, no one will ever be able to walk over you."

Another example: One day I was impatiently awaiting an important telephone call. I resisted every call that came in and made no out-going calls myself, reasoning that it might interfere with the one I was awaiting.

Instead of saying, "Divine ideas never conflict, the call will come at the right time," leaving it to Infinite Intelligence to arrange, I commenced to manage things myself—I made the battle mine, not God's and remained tense and anxious. The bell did not ring for about an hour, and I glanced at the 'phone and found the receiver had been off that length of time, and the 'phone was disconnected. My anxiety, fear and belief in interference, had brought on a total eclipse of the telephone. Realizing what I had done, I commenced blessing the situation at once; I baptized it "success," and affirmed, "I cannot lose any call that belongs to me by divine right; I am under grace, and not under law."

A friend rushed out to the nearest telephone, to notify the Company to reconnect.

She entered a crowded grocery, but the proprietor left his customers and attended to the call himself. My 'phone was connected at once, and two minutes later, I received a very important call, and about an hour afterward, the one I had been awaiting.

One's ships come in over a calm sea.

So long as man resists a situation, he will have it with him. If he runs away from it, it will run after him.

For example: I repeated this to a woman one day, and she replied, "How true that is! I was unhappy at home, I disliked my mother, who was critical and domineering; so I ran away and was married—but I married my mother, for my husband was exactly like my mother, and I had the same situation to face again." "Agree with thine adversary quickly."

That means, agree that the adverse situation is good, be undisturbed by it, and it falls away of its own weight. "None of these things move me," is a wonderful affirmation.

The inharmonious situation comes from some inharmony within man himself.

When there is, in him, no emotional response to an inharmonious situation, it fades away forever, from his pathway.

So we see man's work is ever with himself.

People have said to me, "Give treatments to change my husband, or my brother." I reply, "No, I will give *treatments to change you;* when you change, your husband and your brother will change."

One of my students was in the habit of lying. I told her it was a failure method and if she lied, she would be lied to. She replied, "I don't care, I can't possibly get along without lying."

One day she was speaking on the 'phone to a man with whom she was very much in love. She turned to me and said, "I don't trust him, I know he's lying to me." I replied, "Well, you lie yourself, so someone has to lie to you, and you will be sure it will be just the person you want the truth from." Some time after that, I saw her, and she said, "I'm cured of lying."

I questioned: "What cured you?"

She replied: "I have been living with a woman who lied worse than I did!"

One is often cured of his faults by seeing them in others.

Life is a mirror, and we find only ourselves reflected in our associates.

Living in the past is a failure method and a violation of spiritual law.

Jesus Christ said, "Behold, now is the accepted time." "Now is the day of Salvation."

Lot's wife looked back and was turned into a pillar of salt.

The robbers of time are the past and the future. Man should bless the past, and forget it, if it keeps him in bondage, and bless the future, knowing it has in store for him endless joys, but live *fully in the now.*

For example: A woman came to me, complaining that she had no money with which to buy Christmas gifts. She said, "Last year was so different; I had plenty of money and gave lovely presents, and this year I have scarcely a cent."

I replied, "You will never demonstrate money while you are pathetic and live in the past. Live fully in the *now,* and *get ready to give Christmas presents.* Dig your ditches, and the money will come." She exclaimed, "I know what to do! I will buy some tinsel twine, Christmas seals and wrapping paper." I replied, "Do that, and the *presents will come and stick themselves to the Christmas seals.*"

This too, was showing financial fearlessness and faith in God, as the reasoning mind said, "Keep every cent you have, as you are not sure you will get any more."

She bought the seals, paper and twine, and a few days before Christmas, received a gift of several hundred dollars. Buying the seals and twine had impressed the subconscious with expectancy, and opened the way for the manifestation of the money. She purchased all the presents in plenty of time.

Man must live suspended in the moment.

"Look well, therefore, to this Day! Such is the salutation of the Dawn."

He must be spiritually alert, ever awaiting his leads, taking advantage of every opportunity.

One day, I said continually (silently), "Infinite Spirit, don't let me miss a trick," and something very important was told to me that evening. It is most necessary to begin the day with right words.

Make an affirmation immediately upon waking.

For example:

"Thy will be done this day! Today is a day of completion; I give thanks for this perfect day, miracle shall follow miracle and wonders shall never cease."

Make this a habit, and one will see wonders and miracles come into his life.

One morning I picked up a book and read, "Look with wonder at that which is before you!" It seemed to be my message for the day, so I repeated again and again, "Look with wonder at that which is before you."

At about noon, a large sum of money, was given me, which I had been desiring for a certain purpose.

In a following chapter, I will give affirmations that I have found most effective. However, one should never use an affirmation unless it is absolutely satisfying and convincing to his own consciousness, and often an affirmative is changed to suit different people.

For example: The following has brought success to many:

"I have a wonderful work, in a wonderful way, I give wonderful service, for wonderful pay!"

I gave the first two lines to one of my students, and she added the last two.

It made *a most powerful statement*, as there should always be perfect payment for perfect service, and a rhyme sinks easily into the subconscious. She went about singing it aloud and soon did receive wonderful work in a wonderful way, and gave wonderful service for wonderful pay.

Another student, a business man, took it, and changed the word work to business.

He repeated, "I have a wonderful business, in a wonderful way, and I give wonderful service for wonderful pay." That afternoon he made a forty-one-thousand dollar deal, though there had been no activity in his affairs for months.

Every affirmation must be carefully worded and completely "cover the ground."

For example: I knew a woman, who was in great need, and made a demand for work. She received a great deal of work, but was never paid anything. She now knows to add, "wonderful service for wonderful pay."

It is man's divine right to have plenty! More than enough!

"His barns should be full, and his cup should flow over!" This is God's idea for man, and when man breaks down the barriers of lack in his own consciousness, the Golden Age will be his, and every righteous desire of his heart fulfilled!

V

THE LAW OF KARMA
AND
THE LAW OF FORGIVENESS

Man receives only that which he gives. The Game of Life is a game of boomerangs. Man's thoughts, deeds and words, return to him sooner or later, with astounding accuracy.

This is the law of Karma, which is Sanskrit for "Comeback." "Whatsoever a man soweth, that shall he also reap."

For example: A friend told me this story of herself, illustrating the law. She said, "I make all my Karma on my aunt, whatever I say to her, someone says to me. I am often irritable at home, and one day, said to my aunt, who was talking to me during dinner. '*No more talk, I wish to eat in peace.*'"

"The following day, I was lunching with a woman with whom I wished to make a great impression. I was talking animatedly, when she said: '*No more talk, I wish to eat in peace!*'"

My friend is high in consciousness, so her Karma returns much more quickly than to one on the mental plane.

The more man knows, the more he is responsible for, and a person with a knowledge of Spiritual Law, which he does not practice, suffers greatly, in consequence. "The fear of the Lord (law) is the beginning of wisdom." If we read the word Lord, law, it will make many passages in the Bible much clearer.

"Vengeance is mine, I will repay, saith the Lord" (law). It is the law which takes vengeance, not God. God sees man perfect, "created in his own image," (imagination) and given "power and dominion."

This is the perfect idea of man, registered in Divine Mind, awaiting man's recognition; for man can only be what he sees himself to be, and only attain what he sees himself attaining.

"Nothing ever happens without an on-looker" is an ancient saying.

Man sees first his failure or success, his joy or sorrow, before it swings into visibility from the scenes set in his own imagination. We have observed this in the mother picturing disease for her child, or a woman seeing success for her husband.

Jesus Christ said, "And ye shall know the truth and the truth shall make you free."

So, we see freedom (from all unhappy conditions) comes through knowledge—a knowledge of Spiritual Law.

Obedience precedes authority, and the law obeys man when he obeys the law. The law of electricity must be obeyed before it becomes man's servant. When handled ignorantly, it becomes man's deadly foe. *So with the laws of Mind!*

For example: A woman with a strong personal will, wished she owned a house which belonged to an acquaintance, and she often made mental pictures of herself living in the house. In the course of time, the man died and she moved into the house. Several years afterwards, coming into the knowledge of Spiritual Law, she said to me: "Do you think I had anything to do with that man's death?" I replied: "Yes, your desire was so strong, everything made way for it, but you paid your Karmic debt. Your husband, whom you loved devotedly, died soon after, and the house was a white elephant on your hands for years."

The original owner, however, could not have been affected by her thoughts had he been positive in the truth, nor her husband, but they were both under Karmic law. The woman should have said (feeling the great desire for the house), "Infinite Intelligence, give me the right house, equally as charming as this, the house *which is mine by divine right*."

The divine selection would have given perfect satisfaction and brought good to all. The divine pattern is the only safe pattern to work by.

Desire is a tremendous force, and must be directed in the right channels, or chaos ensues.

In demonstrating, the most important step is the *first step*, to "*ask aright*."

Man should always demand only that which is his by *divine right*.

To go back to the illustration: Had the woman taken this attitude: "If this house, I desire, is mine, I cannot lose it, if it is not, give me its equivalent," the man might have decided to move out, harmoniously (had it been the divine selection for her) or another house would have been substituted. Anything forced into manifestation through personal will, is always "ill-got," and has "ever bad success."

Man is admonished, "My will be done not thine," and the curious thing is, man always gets just what he desires when he does relinquish personal will, thereby enabling Infinite Intelligence to work through him.

"Stand ye still and see the salvation of the Lord" (law).

For example: A woman came to me in great distress. Her daughter had determined to take a very hazardous trip, and the mother was filled with fear.

She said she had used every argument, had pointed out the dangers to be encountered, and forbidden her to go, but the daughter became more and more rebellious and determined. I said to the mother, "You are forcing your personal will upon your daughter, which you have no right to do, and your fear of the trip is only attracting it, for man attracts what he fears." I added, "Let go, and take your mental hands off; *put it in God's Hands, and use this statement:*" "I put this situation in the hands of Infinite Love and Wisdom; if this trip is the Divine plan, I bless it and no longer resist, but if it is not divinely planned, I give thanks that it is now dissolved and dissipated." A day or two after that, her daughter said to her, "Mother, I have given up the trip," and the situation returned to its "native nothingness."

It is learning to "stand still," which seems so difficult for man. I will deal more fully with this law in the chapter on non-resistance.

I will give another example of sowing and reaping, which came in the most curious way.

A woman came to me saying, she had received a counterfeit twenty-dollar bill, given to her at the bank. She was much disturbed, for, she said, "The people at the bank will never acknowledge their mistake."

I replied, "Let us analyze the situation and find out why you attracted it." She thought a few moments and exclaimed: "I know it, I sent a friend a lot of stagemoney, just for a joke." So the law had sent her some stagemoney, for it doesn't know anything about jokes.

I said, "Now we will call on the law of forgiveness, and neutralize the situation."

Christianity is founded upon the law of forgiveness—Christ has redeemed us from the curse of the Karmic law, and the Christ within each man is his Redeemer and Salvation from all inharmonious conditions.

So I said: "Infinite Spirit, we call on the law of forgiveness and give thanks that she is under grace and not under law, and cannot lose this twenty dollars which is hers by divine right."

"Now," I said, "Go back to the bank and tell them, fearlessly, that it was given you, there by mistake."

She obeyed, and to her surprise, they apologized and gave her another bill, treating her most courteously.

So knowledge of the Law gives man power to "rub out his mistakes." Man cannot force the external to be what he is not.

If he desires riches, he must be rich first in consciousness.

For example: A woman came to me asking treatment for prosperity. She did not take much interest in her household affairs, and her home was in great disorder.

I said to her, "If you wish to be rich, you must be orderly. All men with great wealth are orderly—and order is heaven's first law." I added, "You will never become rich with a burnt match in the pincushion."

She had a good sense of humor and commenced immediately, putting her house in order. She rearranged furniture, straightened out bureau drawers, cleaned rugs, and soon made a big financial demonstration—a gift from a relative. The woman, herself, became made over, and keeps herself keyed-up financially, by being ever watchful of the *external and expecting prosperity, knowing God is her supply.*

Many people are in ignorance of the fact that gifts and things are investments, and that hoarding and saving invariably lead to loss.

"There is that scattereth and yet increaseth; and there is that withholdeth more than is meet, but it tendeth to poverty."

For example: I knew a man who wanted to buy a fur-lined overcoat. He and his wife went to various shops, but there was none he wanted. He said they were all too cheap-looking. At last, he was shown one, the salesman said was valued at a thousand dollars, but which the manager would sell him for five-hundred dollars, as it was late in the season.

His financial possessions amounted to about seven hundred dollars. The reasoning mind would have said, "You can't afford to spend nearly all you have on a coat," but he was very intuitive and never reasoned.

He turned to his wife and said, "If I get this coat, I'll make a ton of money!" So his wife consented, weakly.

About a month later, he received a ten-thousand-dollar commission. The coat made him feel so rich, it linked him with success and prosperity; without the coat, he would not have received the commission. It was an investment paying large dividends!

If man ignores these leadings to spend or to give, the same amount of money will go in an uninteresting or unhappy way.

For example: A woman told me, on Thanksgiving Day, she informed her family that they could not afford a Thanksgiving dinner. She had the money, but decided to save it.

A few days later, someone entered her room and took from the bureau drawer the exact amount the dinner would have cost.

The law always stands back of the man who spends fearlessly, with wisdom.

For example: One of my students was shopping with her little nephew. The child clamored for a toy, which she told him she could not afford to buy.

She realized suddenly that she was seeking lack, and not recognizing God as her supply!

So she bought the toy, and on her way home, *picked up, in the street, the exact amount of money she had paid for it.*

Man's supply is inexhaustible and unfailing when fully trusted, but faith or trust must precede the demonstration. "According to your faith be it unto you." "Faith is the substance of things hoped for, the evidence of things not seen—" for faith holds the vision steady, and the adverse pictures are dissolved and dissipated, and "in due season we shall reap, if we faint not."

Jesus Christ brought the good news (the gospel) that there was a higher law than the law of Karma—and that that law transcends the law of Karma. It is the law of grace, or forgiveness. It is the law which *frees man from the law of cause and effect—the law of consequence. "Under grace, and not under law."*

We are told that on this plane, man reaps where he has not sown; the gifts of God are simply poured out upon him. "All that the Kingdom affords is his." This continued state of bliss awaits the man who has overcome the race (or world) thought.

In the world thought there is tribulation, but Jesus Christ said: "Be of good cheer; I have overcome the world."

The world thought is that of sin, sickness and death. He saw their absolute unreality and said sickness and sorrow shall pass away and death itself, the last enemy, be overcome.

We know now, from a scientific standpoint, that death could be overcome by stamping the subconscious mind with the conviction of eternal youth and eternal life.

The subconscious, being simply power without direction, *carries out orders without questioning.*

Working under the direction of the superconscious (the Christ or God within man) the "resurrection of the body" would be accomplished.

Man would no longer throw off his body in death, it would be transformed into the "body electric," sung by Walt Whitman, for Christianity is founded upon the forgiveness of sins and "an empty tomb."

CASTING THE BURDEN

IMPRESSING THE SUBCONSCIOUS

When man knows his own powers and the workings of his mind, his great desire is to find an easy and quick way to impress the subconscious with good, for simply an intellectual knowledge of the Truth will not bring results.

In my own case, I found the easiest way is in "casting the burden."

A metaphysician once explained it in this manner. He said, "The only thing which gives anything weight in nature, is the law of gravitation, and if a boulder could be taken high above the planet, there would be no weight in that boulder; and that is what Jesus Christ meant when he said: "My yoke is easy and my burden is light."

He had overcome the world vibration, and functioned in the fourth dimensional realm, where there is only perfection, completion, life and joy.

He said: "Come to me all ye that labor and are heavy laden, and I will give you rest." "Take my yoke upon you, for my yoke is easy and my burden is light."

We are also told in the fifty-fifth Psalm, to "cast thy burden upon the Lord." Many passages in the Bible state that the *battle* is God's not man's and that man is always to "*stand still*" *and see the Salvation of the Lord.*

This indicates that the superconscious mind (or Christ within) is the department which fights man's battle and relieves him of burdens.

We see, therefore, that man violates law if he carries a burden, and a burden is an adverse thought or condition, and this thought or condition has its root in the subconscious.

It seems almost impossible to make any headway directing the subconscious from the conscious, or reasoning mind, as the reasoning mind (the intellect) is limited in its conceptions, and filled with doubts and fears.

How scientific it then is, to cast the burden upon the superconscious mind (or Christ within) where it is "made light," or dissolved into its "native nothingness."

For example: A woman in urgent need of money, "made light" upon the Christ within, the superconscious, with the statement, "I cast this burden of lack on the Christ (within) and I go free to have plenty!"

The belief in lack was her burden, and as she cast it upon the Superconscious with its belief of plenty, an avalanche of supply was the result.

We read, "The Christ in you the hope of glory."

Another example: One of my students had been given a new piano, and there was no room in her studio for it until she had moved out the old one. She was in a state of perplexity. She wanted to keep the old piano, but knew of no place to send it. She became desperate, as the new piano was to be sent immediately; in fact, was on its way, with no place to put it. She said it came to her to repeat, "I cast this burden on the Christ within, and I go free."

A few moments later, her 'phone rang, and a woman friend asked if she might rent her old piano, and it was moved out, a few minutes before the new one arrived.

I knew a woman, whose burden was resentment. She said, "I cast this burden of resentment on the Christ within, and I go free, to be loving, harmonious and happy." The Almighty superconscious, flooded the subconscious with love, and her whole life was changed. For years, resentment had held her in a state of torment and imprisoned her soul (the subconscious mind).

The statement should be made over and over and over, sometimes for hours at a time, silently or audibly, with quietness but determination.

I have often compared it to winding-up a victrola. We must wind ourselves up with spoken words.

I have noticed, in "casting the burden," after a little while, one seems to see clearly. It is impossible to have clear vision, while in the throes of carnal mind. Doubts and fear poison the mind and body and imagination runs riot, attracting disaster and disease.

In steadily repeating the affirmation, "I cast this burden on the Christ within, and go free," the vision clears, and with it a feeling of relief, and sooner or later comes *the manifestation of good, be it health, happiness or supply.*

One of my students once asked me to explain the "darkness before the dawn." I referred in a preceding chapter to the fact that often, before the big demonstration "everything seems to go wrong," and deep depression clouds the consciousness. It means that out of the subconscious are rising the doubts and fears of the ages. These old derelicts of the subconscious rise to the surface, to be put out.

It is then, that man should clap his cymbals, like Jehoshaphat, and give thanks that he is saved, even though he seems surrounded by the enemy (the situation of lack or disease). The student continued, "How long must one remain in the dark" and I replied, "until *one can see in the dark,*" and "*casting the burden enables one to see in the dark.*"

In order to impress the subconscious, active faith is always essential.

"Faith without works is dead." In these chapters I have endeavored to bring out this point.

Jesus Christ showed active faith when "He commanded the multitude to sit down on the ground," before he gave thanks for the loaves and the fishes.

I will give another example showing how necessary this step is. In fact, active faith is the bridge, over which man passes to his Promised Land.

Through misunderstanding, a woman had been separated from her husband, whom she loved deeply. He refused all offers of reconciliation and would not communicate with her in any way.

Coming into the knowledge of Spiritual law, she denied the appearance of separation. She made this statement: "There is no separation in Divine Mind, therefore, I cannot be separated from the love and companionship which are mine by divine right."

She showed active faith by arranging a place for him at the table every day; thereby impressing the subconscious with a picture of his *return*. Over a year passed, but she never wavered, and *one day he walked in.*

The subconscious is often impressed through music. Music has a fourth dimensional quality and releases the soul from imprisonment. It makes wonderful things seem *possible, and easy of accomplishment!*

I have a friend who uses her victrola, daily, for this purpose. It puts her in perfect harmony and releases the imagination.

Another woman often dances while making her affirmations. The rhythm and harmony of music and motion carry her words forth with tremendous power.

The student must remember also, not to despise the "day of small things."

Invariably, before a demonstration, come "signs of land."

Before Columbus reached America, he saw birds and twigs which showed him land was near. So it is with a demonstration; but often the student mistakes it for the demonstration itself, and is disappointed.

For example: A woman had "spoken the word" for a set of dishes. Not long afterwards a friend gave her a dish which was old and cracked.

She came to me and said, "Well, I asked for a set of dishes, and all I got was a cracked plate."

I replied, "The plate was only signs of land. It shows your dishes are coming—look upon it as birds and seaweed," and not long afterwards the dishes came.

Continually "making-believe," impresses the subconscious. If one makes believe he is rich, and makes believe he is successful, in "due time he will reap."

Children are always "making believe," and "except ye be converted, and become as little children, ye shall not enter the Kingdom of Heaven."

For example: I know of a woman who was very poor, but no one could make her *feel poor*. She earned a small amount of money from rich friends, who constantly reminded her of her poverty, and to be careful and saving. Regardless of their admonitions, she would spend all her earnings on a hat, or make someone a gift, and be in a rapturous state of mind. Her thoughts were always centered on beautiful clothes and "rings and things," but without envying others.

She lived in the world of the wondrous, and only riches seemed real to her. Before long she married a rich man, and the rings and things became visible. I do not know whether the man was the "Divine Selection," but opulence had to manifest in her life, as she had imaged only opulence.

There is no peace or happiness for man, until he has erased all fear from the subconscious.

Fear is misdirected energy and must be redirected, or transmuted into Faith.

Jesus Christ said, "Why are ye fearful, O ye of little faith?" "All things are possible to him that believeth."

I am asked, so often by my students, "*How can I get rid of fear?*"

I reply, "*By walking up to the thing you are afraid of.*"

"The lion takes its fierceness from your fear."

Walk up to the lion, and he will disappear; run away and he runs after you.

I have shown in previous chapters, how the lion of lack disappeared when the individual spent money fearlessly, showing faith that God was his supply and therefore, unfailing.

Many of my students have come out of the bondage of poverty, and are now bountifully supplied, through losing all fear of letting money go out. The subconscious is impressed with the truth that *God is the Giver and the Gift;* therefore as one is one with the Giver, he is one with the Gift. A splendid statement is, "I now thank God the Giver for God the Gift."

Man has so long separated himself from his good and his supply, through thoughts of separation and lack, that sometimes, it takes dynamite to dislodge these false ideas from the subconscious, and the dynamite is a big situation.

We see in the foregoing illustration, how the individual was freed from his bondage by *showing fearlessness.*

Man should watch himself hourly to detect if his motive for action is fear or faith.

"Choose ye this day whom we shall serve," fear or faith.

Perhaps one's fear is of personality. Then do not avoid the people feared; be willing to meet them cheerfully, and they will either prove "golden links in the chain of one's good," or disappear harmoniously from one's pathway.

Perhaps one's fear is of disease or germs. Then one should be fearless and undisturbed in a germ-laden situation, and he would be immune.

One can only contract germs while vibrating at the same rate as the germ, and fear drags men down to the level of the germ. Of course, the disease laden germ is the product of carnal mind, as all thought must objectify. Germs do not exist in the superconscious or Divine Mind, therefore are the product of man's "vain imagination."

"In the twinkling of an eye," man's release will come when he realizes *there is no power in evil.*

The material world will fade away, and the fourth dimensional world, the "World of the Wondrous," will swing into manifestation.

"And I saw a new heaven, and a new earth—and there shall be no more death, neither sorrow nor crying, neither shall there be any more pain; for the former things are passed away."

LOVE

Every man on this planet is taking his initiation in love. "A new commandment I give unto you, that ye love one another." Ouspensky states, in "Tertium Organum," that "love is a cosmic phenomenon," and opens to man the fourth dimensional world, "The World of the Wondrous."

Real love is selfless and free from fear. It pours itself out upon the object of its affection, without demanding any return. Its joy is in the joy of giving. Love is God in manifestation, and the strongest magnetic force in the universe. Pure, unselfish love *draws to itself its own;* it does not need to seek or demand. Scarcely anyone has the faintest conception of real love. Man is selfish, tyrannical or fearful in his affections, thereby losing the thing he loves. Jealousy is the worst enemy of love, for the imagination runs riot, seeing the loved one attracted to another, and invariably these fears objectify if they are not neutralized.

For example: A woman came to me in deep distress. The man she loved had left her for other women, and said he never intended to marry her. She was torn with jealousy and resentment and said she hoped he would suffer as he had made her suffer; and added, "How could he leave me when I loved him so much?"

I replied, "You are not loving that man, you are hating him," and added, "*You can never receive what you have never given. Give a perfect love and you will receive a perfect love.* Perfect yourself on this man. Give him a perfect, *unselfish* love, demanding nothing in return, do not criticise or condemn, and *bless him wherever he is.*"

She replied, "No, I won't bless him unless I know where he is!"

"Well," I said, "that is not real love."

"When you *send out real love,* real love will return to you, either from this man or his equivalent, for if this man is not the divine selection, you will not want him. As you are one with God, you are one with the love which belongs to you by divine right."

Several months passed, and matters remained about the same, but she was working conscientiously with herself. I said, "When you are no longer disturbed by his cruelty, he will cease to be cruel, as you are attracting it through your own emotions."

Then I told her of a brotherhood in India, who never said, "Good morning" to each other. They used these words: "*I salute the Divinity in you.*" They saluted the divinity in every man, and in the wild animals in the jungle, and they were never harmed, for they *saw only God in every* living thing. I said, "Salute the divinity in this man, and say, 'I see your divine self only. I see you as God sees you, perfect, made in His image and likeness.'"

She found she was becoming more poised, and gradually losing her resentment. He was a Captain, and she always called him "The Cap."

One day, she said, suddenly, "*God bless the Cap wherever he is.*"

I replied: "Now, that is real love, and when you have become a 'complete circle,' and are no longer disturbed by the situation, you will have his love, or attract its equivalent."

I was moving at this time, and did not have a telephone, so was out of touch with her for a few weeks, when one morning I received a letter saying, "We are married."

At the earliest opportunity, I paid her a call. My first words were, "What happened?"

"Oh," she exclaimed, "a miracle! One day I woke up and all suffering had ceased. I saw him that evening and he asked me to marry him. We were married in about a week, and I have never seen a more devoted man."

There is an old saying: "*No man is your enemy, no man is your friend, every man is your teacher.*"

So one should become impersonal and learn what each man has to teach him, and soon he would learn his lessons and be free.

The woman's lover was teaching her selfless love, which every man, sooner or later, must learn.

Suffering is not necessary for man's development; it is the result of violation of spiritual law, but few people seem able to rouse themselves from their "soul sleep" without it. When people are happy, they usually become selfish, and automatically the law of Karma is set in action. Man often suffers loss through lack of appreciation.

I knew a woman who had a very nice husband, but she said often, "I don't care anything about being married, but that is nothing against my husband. I'm simply not interested in married life."

She had other interests, and scarcely remembered she had a husband. She only thought of him when she saw him. One day her husband told her he was in love with another woman, and left. She came to me in distress and resentment.

I replied, "It is exactly what you spoke the word for. You said you didn't care anything about being married, so the subconscious worked to get you unmarried."

She said, "Oh yes, I see. People get what they want, and then feel very much hurt."

She soon became in perfect harmony with the situation, and knew they were both much happier apart.

When a woman becomes indifferent or critical, and ceases to be an inspiration to her husband, he misses the stimulus of their early relationship and is restless and unhappy.

A man came to me dejected, miserable and poor. His wife was interested in the "Science of Numbers," and had had him read. It seems the report was not very favorable, for he said, "My wife says I'll never amount to anything because I am a two."

I replied, "I don't care what your number is, you are a perfect idea in divine mind, and we will demand the success and prosperity which are *already planned* for you by that Infinite Intelligence."

Within a few weeks, he had a very fine position, and a year or two later, he achieved a brilliant success as a writer. No man is a success in business unless he loves his work. The picture the artist paints for love (of his art) is his greatest work. The pot-boiler is always something to live down.

No man can attract money if he despises it. Many people are kept in poverty by saying: "Money means nothing to me, and I have a contempt for people who have it."

CHAPTER VII

This is the reason so many artists are poor. Their contempt for money separates them from it.

I remember hearing one artist say of another, "He's no good as an artist, he has money in the bank."

This attitude of mind, of course, separates man from his supply; he must be in harmony with a thing in order to attract it.

Money is God in manifestation, as freedom from want and limitation, but it must be always kept in circulation and put to right uses. Hoarding and saving react with grim vengeance.

This does not mean that man should not have houses and lots, stocks and bonds, for "the barns of the righteous man shall be full." It means man should not hoard even the principal, if an occasion arises, when money is necessary. In letting it go out fearlessly and cheerfully he opens the way for more to come in, for God is man's unfailing and inexhaustible supply.

This is the spiritual attitude towards money and the great Bank of the Universal never fails!

We see an example of hoarding in the film production of "Greed." The woman won five thousand dollars in a lottery, but would not spend it. She hoarded and saved, let her husband suffer and starve, and eventually she scrubbed floors for a living.

She loved the money itself and put it above everything, and one night she was murdered and the money taken from her.

This is an example of where "love of money is the root of all evil." Money in itself, is good and beneficial, but used for destructive purposes, hoarded and saved, or considered more important than love, brings disease and disaster, and the loss of the money itself.

Follow the path of love, and all things are added, *for God is love,* and *God is supply;* follow the path of selfishness and greed, and the supply vanishes, or man is separated from it.

For example; I knew the case of a very rich woman, who hoarded her income. She rarely gave anything away, but bought and bought and bought things for herself.

She was very fond of necklaces, and a friend once asked her how many she possessed. She replied, "Sixty-seven." She bought them and put them away, carefully wrapped in tissue paper. Had she used the necklaces it would have been quite legitimate, but she was violating "the law of use." Her closets were filled with clothes she never wore, and jewels which never saw the light.

The woman's arms were gradually becoming paralyzed from holding on to things, and eventually she was considered incapable of looking after her affairs and her wealth was handed over to others to manage.

So man, in ignorance of the law, brings about his own destruction.

All disease, all unhappiness, come from the violation of the law of love. Man's boomerangs of hate, resentment and criticism, come back laden with sickness and sorrow. Love seems almost a lost art, but the man with the knowledge of spiritual law knows it must be regained, for without it, he has "become as sounding brass and tinkling cymbals."

For example: I had a student who came to me, month after month, to clean her consciousness of resentment. After a while, she arrived at the point where she resented only one woman, but that one woman kept her busy. Little by little she became poised and harmonious, and one day, all resentment was wiped out.

She came in radiant, and exclaimed "You can't understand how I feel! The woman said something to me and instead of being furious I was loving and kind, and she apologized and was perfectly lovely to me.

No one can understand the marvelous lightness I feel within!"

Love and good-will are invaluable in business. For example: A woman came to me, complaining of her employer. She said she was cold and critical and knew she did not want her in the position.

"Well," I replied, "Salute the Divinity in the woman and send her love."

She said "I can't; she's a marble woman."

I answered, "You remember the story of the sculptor who asked for a certain piece of marble. He was asked why he wanted it, and he replied, 'because there is an angel in the marble,' and out of it he produced a wonderful work of art."

She said, "Very well, I'll try it." A week later she came back and said, "I did what you told me to, and now the woman is very kind, and took me out in her car."

People are sometimes filled with remorse for having done someone an unkindness, perhaps years ago.

If the wrong cannot be righted, its effect can be neutralized by doing some one a kindness *in the present.*

"This one thing I do, forgetting those things which are behind and reaching forth unto those things which are before."

Sorrow, regret and remorse tear down the cells of the body, and poison the atmosphere of the individual.

A woman said to me in deep sorrow, "Treat me to be happy and joyous, for my sorrow makes me so irritable with the members of my family that I keep making more Karma."

I was asked to treat a woman who was mourning for her daughter. I denied all belief in loss and separation, and affirmed that God was the woman's joy, love and peace.

The woman gained her poise at once, but sent word by her son, not to treat any longer, because she was "so happy, it wasn't respectable."

So "mortal mind" loves to hang on to its griefs and regrets.

I knew a woman who went about bragging of her troubles, so, of course, she always had something to brag about.

The old idea was if a woman did not worry about her children, she was not a good mother.

Now, we know that mother-fear is responsible for many of the diseases and accidents which come into the lives of children.

For fear pictures vividly the disease or situation feared, and these pictures objectify, if not neutralized.

Happy is the mother who can say sincerely, that she puts her child in God's hands, and knows therefore, that he is divinely protected.

For example: A woman awoke suddenly, in the night, feeling her brother was in great danger. Instead of giving in to her fears, she commenced making statements of Truth, saying, "Man is a perfect idea in Divine Mind, and is always in his right place, therefore, my brother is in his right place, and is divinely protected."

CHAPTER VII

The next day she found that her brother had been in close proximity to an explosion in a mine, but had miraculously escaped.

So man is his brother's keeper (in thought) and every man should know that the thing he loves dwells in "the secret place of the most high, and abides under the shadow of the Almighty."

"There shall no evil befall thee, neither shall any plague come nigh thy dwelling."

"Perfect love casteth out fear. He that feareth is not made perfect in love," and *"Love is the fulfilling of the Law."*

VIII

INTUITION OR GUIDANCE

"In all thy ways acknowledge Him and He shall direct thy paths."

There is nothing too great of accomplishment for the man who knows the power of his word, and who follows his intuitive leads. By the word he starts in action unseen forces and can rebuild his body or remold his affairs.

It is, therefore, of the utmost importance to choose the right words, and the student carefully selects the affirmation he wishes to catapult into the invisible.

He knows that God is his supply, that there is a supply for every demand, and that his spoken word releases this supply.

"Ask and ye shall receive."

Man must make the first move. "Draw nigh to God and He will draw nigh to you."

I have often been asked just how to make a demonstration.

I reply: "Speak the word and then do not do anything until you get a definite lead." Demand the lead, saying, "Infinite Spirit, reveal to me the way, let me know if there is anything for me to do."

The answer will come through intuition (or hunch); a chance remark from someone, or a passage in a book, etc., etc.

The answers are sometimes quite startling in their exactness. For example: A woman desired a large sum of money. She spoke the words: "Infinite Spirit, open the way for my immediate supply, let all that is mine by divine right now reach me, in great avalanches of abundance." Then she added: "Give me a definite lead, let me know if there is anything for me to do."

The thought came quickly, "Give a certain friend" (who had helped her spiritually) "a hundred dollars." She told her friend, who said, "Wait and get another lead, before giving it." So she waited, and that day met a woman who said to her, "I gave someone a dollar today; it was just as much for me, as it would be for you to give someone a hundred."

This was indeed an unmistakable lead, so she knew she was right in giving the hundred dollars. It was a gift which proved a great investment, for shortly after that, a large sum of money came to her in a remarkable way.

Giving opens the way for receiving. In order to create activity in finances, one should give. Tithing or giving one-tenth of one's income, is an old Jewish custom, and is sure to bring increase. Many of the richest men in this country have been tithers, and I have never known it to fail as an investment.

The tenth-part goes forth and returns blessed and multiplied. But the gift or tithe must be given with love and cheerfulness, for "God loveth a cheerful giver." Bills should be paid cheerfully; all money should be sent forth fearlessly and with a blessing.

This attitude of mind makes man master of money. It is his to obey, and his spoken word then opens vast reservoirs of wealth.

CHAPTER VIII

Man, himself, limits his supply by his limited vision. Sometimes the student has a great realization of wealth, but is afraid to act.

The vision and action must go hand in hand, as in the case of the man who bought the fur-lined overcoat.

A woman came to me asking me to "speak the word" for a position. So I demanded: "Infinite Spirit, open the way for this woman's right position." Never ask for just "a position"; ask for the right position, the place already planned in Divine Mind, as it is the only one that will give satisfaction.

I then gave thanks that she had already received, and that it would manifest quickly. Very soon, she had three positions offered her, two in New York and one in Palm Beach, and she did not know which to choose. I said, "Ask for a definite lead."

The time was almost up and was still undecided, when one day, she telephoned, "When I woke up this morning, I could smell Palm Beach." She had been there before and knew its balmy fragrance.

I replied: "Well, if you can smell Palm Beach from here, it is certainly your lead." She accepted the position, and it proved a great success. Often one's lead comes at an unexpected time.

One day, I was walking down the street, when I suddenly felt a strong urge to go to a certain bakery, a block or two away.

The reasoning mind resisted, arguing, "There is nothing there that you want."

However, I had learned not to reason, so I went to the bakery, looked at everything, and there was certainly nothing there that I wanted, but coming out I encountered a woman I had thought of often, and who was in great need of the help which I could give her.

So often, one goes for one thing and finds another.

Intuition is a spiritual faculty and does not explain, but simply *points the way*.

A person often receives a lead during a "treatment." The idea that comes may seem quite irrelevant, but some of God's leadings are "mysterious."

In the class, one day, I was treating that each individual would receive a definite lead. A woman came to me afterwards, and said: "While you were treating, I got the hunch to take my furniture out of storage and get an apartment." The woman had come to be treated for health. I told her I knew in getting a home of her own, her health would improve, and I added, "I believe your trouble, which is a congestion, has come from having things stored away. Congestion of things causes congestion in the body. You have violated the law of use, and your body is paying the penalty."

So I gave thanks that *"Divine order was established in her mind, body and affairs."*

People little dream of how their affairs react on the body. There is a mental correspondence for every disease. A person might receive instantaneous healing through the realization of his body being a perfect idea in Divine Mind, and, therefore, whole and perfect, but if he continues his destructive thinking, hoarding, hating, fearing, condemning, the disease will return.

Jesus Christ knew that all sickness came from sin, but admonished the leper after the healing, to go and sin no more, lest a worse thing come upon him.

So man's soul (or subconscious mind) must be washed whiter than snow, for permanent healing; and the metaphysician is always delving deep for the "correspondence."

Jesus Christ said, "Condemn not lest ye also be condemned."

"Judge not, lest ye be judged."

Many people have attracted disease and unhappiness through condemnation of others.

What man condemns in others, he attracts to himself.

For example: A friend came to me in anger and distress, because her husband had deserted her for another woman. She condemned the other woman, and said continually, "She knew he was a married man, and had no right to accept his attentions."

I replied. "Stop condemning the woman, bless her, and be through with the situation, otherwise, you are attracting the same thing to yourself."

She was deaf to my words, and a year or two later, became deeply interested in a married man, herself.

Man picks up a live-wire whenever he criticises or condemns, and may expect a shock.

Indecision is a stumbling-block in many a pathway. In order to overcome it, make the statement, repeatedly, "*I am always under direct inspiration; I make right decisions, quickly.*"

These words impress the subconscious, and soon one finds himself awake and alert, making his right moves without hesitation. I have found it destructive to look to the psychic plane for guidance, as it is the plane of many minds and not "The One Mind."

As man opens his mind to subjectivity, he becomes a target for destructive forces. The psychic plane is the result of man's mortal thought, and is on the "plane of opposites." He may receive either good or bad messages.

The science of numbers and the reading of horoscopes, keep man down on the mental (or mortal) plane, for they deal only with the Karmic path.

I know of a man who should have been dead, years ago, according to his horoscope, but he is alive and a leader of one of the biggest movements in this country for the uplift of humanity.

It takes a very strong mind to neutralize a prophecy of evil. The student should declare, "Every false prophecy shall come to naught; every plan my Father in heaven has not planned, shall be dissolved and dissipated, the divine idea now comes to pass."

However, if any good message has ever been given one, of coming happiness, or wealth, harbor and expect it, and it will manifest sooner or later, through the law of expectancy.

Man's will should be used to back the universal will. "I will that the will of God be done."

It is God's will to give every man, every righteous desire of his heart, and man's will should be used to hold the perfect vision, without wavering.

The prodigal son said: "I will arise and go to my Father."

It is, indeed, often an effort of the will to leave the husks and swine of mortal thinking. It is so much easier, for the average person, to have fear than faith; *so faith is an effort of the will.*

As man becomes spiritually awakened he recognizes that any external inharmony is the correspondence of mental inharmony. If he stumbles or falls, he may know he is stumbling or falling in consciousness.

One day, a student was walking along the street condemning someone in her thoughts. She was saying, mentally, "That woman is the most disagreeable woman on earth," when suddenly three boy scouts rushed around the corner and almost knocked her over. She did not condemn the boy scouts, but immediately called on the law of forgiveness, and "saluted the divinity" in the woman. Wisdom's way are ways of pleasantness and all her paths are peace.

When one has made his demands upon the Universal, he must be ready for surprises. Everything may seem to be going wrong, when in reality, it is going right.

For example: A woman was told that there was no loss in divine mind, therefore, she could not lose anything which belonged to her; anything lost, would be returned, or she would receive its equivalent.

Several years previously, she had lost two thousand dollars. She had loaned the money to a relative during her lifetime, but the relative had died, leaving no mention of it in her will. The woman was resentful and angry, and as she had no written statement of the transaction, she never received the money, so she determined to deny the loss, and collect the two thousand dollars from the Bank of the Universal. She had to begin by forgiving the woman, as resentment and unforgiveness close the doors of this wonderful bank.

She made this statement, "I deny loss, there is no loss in Divine Mind, therefore, I cannot lose the two thousand dollars, which belong to me by divine right. *As one door shuts another door opens.*"

She was living in an apartment house which was for sale; and in the lease was a clause, stating that if the house was sold, the tenants would be required to move out within ninety days.

Suddenly, the landlord broke the leases and raised the rent. Again, injustice was on her pathway, but this time she was undisturbed. She blessed the landlord, and said, "As the rent has been raised, it means that I'll be that much richer, for God is my supply."

New leases were made out for the advanced rent, but by some divine mistake, the ninety days clause had been forgotten. Soon after, the landlord had an opportunity to sell the house. On account of the mistake in the new leases, the tenants held possession for another year.

The agent offered each tenant two hundred dollars if he would vacate. Several families moved; three remained, including the woman. A month or two passed, and the agent again appeared. This time he said to the woman, "Will you break your lease for the sum of fifteen hundred dollars?" It flashed upon her, "Here comes the two thousand dollars." She remembered having said to friends in the house, "We will all act together if anything more is said about leaving." So her *lead* was to consult her friends.

These friends said: "Well, if they have offered you fifteen hundred they will certainly give two thousand." So she received a check for two thousand dollars for giving up the apartment. It was certainly a remarkable working of the law, and the apparent injustice was merely opening the way for her demonstration.

Chapter VIII

It proved that there is no loss, and when man takes his spiritual stand, he collects all that is his from this great Reservoir of Good.

"I will restore to you the years the locusts have eaten."

The locusts are the doubts, fears, resentments and regrets of mortal thinking.

These adverse thoughts, alone, rob man; for "No man gives to himself but himself, and no man takes away from himself, but himself."

Man is here to prove God and "to bear witness to the truth," and he can only prove God by bringing plenty out of lack, and justice out of injustice.

"Prove me now herewith, saith the Lord of hosts, if I will not open you the windows of heaven, and pour out a blessing, that there shall not be room enough to receive it."

IX

PERFECT SELF-EXPRESSION
OR
THE DIVINE DESIGN

"No wind can drive my bark astray nor change the tide of destiny."

There is for each man, perfect self-expression. There is a place which he is to fill and no one else can fill, something which he is to do, which no one else can do; it is his destiny!

This achievement is held, a perfect idea in Divine Mind, awaiting man's recognition. As the imaging faculty is the creative faculty, it is necessary for man to see the idea, before it can manifest.

So man's highest demand is for the *Divine Design of his life*.

He may not have the faintest conception of what it is, for there is, possibly, some marvelous talent, hidden deep within him.

His demand should be: "*Infinite Spirit, open the way for the Divine Design of my life to manifest; let the genius within me now be released; let me see clearly the perfect plan*."

The perfect plan includes health, wealth, love and perfect self-expression. This is the *square of life*, which brings perfect happiness. When one has made this demand, he may find great changes taking place in his life, for nearly every man has wandered far from the Divine Design.

I know, in one woman's case, it was as though a cyclone had struck her affairs, but readjustments came quickly, and new and wonderful conditions took the place of old ones.

Perfect self-expression will never be labor; but of such absorbing interest that it will seem almost like play. The student knows, also, as man comes into the world financed by God, the *supply* needed for his perfect self-expression will be at hand.

Many a genius has struggled for years with the problem of supply, when his spoken word, and faith, would have released quickly, the necessary funds.

For example: After the class, one day, a man came to me and handed me a cent.

He said: "I have just seven cents in the world, and I'm going to give you one; for I have faith in the power of your spoken word. I want you to speak the word for my perfect self-expression and prosperity."

I "spoke the word," and did not see him again until a year later. He came in one day, successful and happy, with a roll of yellow bills in his pocket. He said, "Immediately after you spoke the word, I had a position offered me in a distant city, and am now demonstrating health, happiness and supply."

A woman's perfect self-expression may be in becoming a perfect wife, a perfect mother, a perfect home-maker and not necessarily in having a public career.

Demand definite leads, and the way will be made easy and successful.

One should not visualize or force a mental picture. When he demands the Divine Design to come into his conscious mind, he will receive flashes of inspiration, and begin to see himself making some great accomplishment. This is the picture, or idea, he must hold without wavering.

The thing man seeks is seeking him—*the telephone was seeking Bell!*

Parents should never force careers and professions upon their children. With a knowledge of spiritual Truth, the Divine Plan could be spoken for, early in childhood, or prenatally.

A prenatal treatment should be: "Let the God in this child have perfect expression; let the Divine Design of his mind, body and affairs be made manifest throughout his life, throughout eternity."

God's will be done, not man's; God's pattern, not man's pattern, is the command we find running through all the scriptures, and the Bible is a book dealing with the science of the mind. It is a book telling man how to release his soul (or subconscious mind) from bondage.

The battles described are pictures of man waging war against mortal thoughts. "A man's foes shall be they of his own household." Every man is Jehoshaphat, and every man is David, who slays Goliath (mortal thinking) with the little white stone (faith).

So man must be careful that he is not the "wicked and slothful servant" who buried his talent. There is a terrible penalty to be paid for not using one's ability.

Often fear stands between man and his perfect self-expression. Stage-fright has hampered many a genius. This may be overcome by the spoken word, or treatment. The individual then loses all self-consciousness, and feels simply that he is a channel for Infinite Intelligence to express Itself through.

He is under direct inspiration, fearless, and confident; for he feels that it is the "Father within" him who does the work.

A young boy came often to my class with his mother. He asked me to "speak the word" for his coming examinations at school.

I told him to make the statement: "I am one with Infinite Intelligence. I know everything I should know on this subject." He had an excellent knowledge of history, but was not sure of his arithmetic. I saw him afterwards, and he said: "I spoke the word for my arithmetic, and passed with the highest honors; but thought I could depend on myself for history, and got a very poor mark." Man often receives a set-back when he is "too sure of himself," which means he is trusting to his personality and not the "Father within."

Another one of my students gave me an example of this. She took an extended trip abroad one summer, visiting many countries, where she was ignorant of the languages. She was calling for guidance and protection every minute, and her affairs went smoothly and miraculously. Her luggage was never delayed nor lost! Accommodations were always ready for her at the best hotels; and she had perfect service wherever she went. She returned to New York. Knowing the language, she felt God was no longer necessary, so looked after her affairs in an ordinary manner.

Everything went wrong, her trunks delayed, amid inharmony and confusion. The student must form the habit of "practicing the Presence of God" every minute. "*In all thy ways acknowledge him,*" nothing is too small or too great.

Sometimes an insignificant incident may be the turning point in a man's life.

Robert Fulton, watching some boiling water, simmering in a tea kettle, saw a steamboat!

I have seen a student, often, keep back his demonstration, through resistance, or pointing the way.

He pins his faith to one channel only, and dictates just the way he desires the manifestation to come, which brings things to a standstill.

"*My way, not your way!*" is the command of Infinite Intelligence. Like all Power, be it steam or electricity, it must have a nonresistant engine or instrument to work through, and man is that engine or instrument.

Over and over again, man is told to "stand still". "Oh Judah, fear not; but tomorrow go out against them, for the Lord will be with you. You shall not need to fight this battle; set yourselves, stand ye still, and see the salvation of the Lord with you."

We see this in the incidents of the two thousand dollars coming to the woman through the landlord when she became *nonresistant* and *undisturbed,* and the woman who won the man's love "after all suffering had ceased."

The student's goal is *Poise! Poise is Power,* for it gives God-Power a chance to rush through man, to "will and to do Its good pleasure."

Poised, he thinks clearly, and makes "right decisions quickly." "He never misses a trick."

Anger blurs the visions, poisons the blood, is the root of many diseases, and causes wrong decision leading to failure.

It has been named one of the worst "sins," as its reaction is so harmful. The student learns that in metaphysics sin has a much broader meaning than in the old teaching. "Whatsoever is not of faith is sin."

He finds that fear and worry are deadly sins. They are inverted faith, and through distorted mental pictures, bring to pass the thing he fears. His work is to drive out these enemies (from the subconscious mind). "When Man is *fearless he is finished!*" Maeterlinck says, that "Man is God afraid."

So, as we read in the previous chapters: Man can only vanquish fear by walking up to the thing he is afraid of. When Jehoshaphat and his army prepared to meet the enemy, singing "Praise the Lord, for his mercy endureth forever," they found their enemies had destroyed each other, and there was nothing to fight.

For example: A woman asked a friend to deliver a message to another friend. The woman feared to give the message, as the reasoning mind said, "Don't get mixed-up in this affair, don't give that message."

She was troubled in spirit, for she had given her promise. At last, she determined to "walk up to the lion," and call on the law of divine protection. She met the friend to whom she was to deliver the message. She opened her mouth to speak it, when her friend said, "So-and-So has left town." This made it unnecessary to give the message, as the situation depended upon the person being in town. As she was willing to do it, she was not obliged to; as she did not fear, the situation vanished.

The student often delays his demonstration through a belief in incompletion. He should make this statement:

"In Divine Mind there is only completion, therefore, my demonstration is completed. My perfect work, my perfect home, my perfect health." Whatever he demands are perfect ideas registered in Divine Mind, and must manifest, "under grace in a perfect way." He gives thanks he has already received on the invisible, and makes active preparation for receiving on the visible.

One of my students was in need of a financial demonstration. She came to me and asked why it was not completed.

I replied: "Perhaps, you are in the habit of leaving things unfinished, and the subconscious has gotten into the habit of not completing (as the without, so the within)."

She said, "You are right. I often *begin things* and never finish them.

"I'll go home and finish something I commenced weeks ago, and I know it will be symbolic of my demonstration."

So she sewed assiduously, and the article was soon completed. Shortly after, the money came in a most curious manner.

Her husband was paid his salary twice that month. He told the people of their mistake, and they sent word to keep it.

When man asks, *believing, he must receive, for God creates His own channels!*

I have been sometimes asked, "Suppose one has several talents, how is he to know which one to choose?" Demand to be shown definitely. Say: "Infinite Spirit, give me a definite lead, reveal to me my perfect self-expression, show me which talent I am to make use of now."

I have known people to suddenly enter a new line of work, and be fully equipped, with little or no training. So make the statement: "*I am fully equipped for the Divine Plan of my life,*" and be fearless in grasping opportunities.

Some people are cheerful givers, but bad receivers. They refuse gifts through pride, or some negative reason, thereby blocking their channels, and invariably find themselves eventually with little or nothing. For example: A woman who had given away a great deal of money, had a gift offered her of several thousand dollars. She refused to take it, saying she did not need it. Shortly after that, her finances were "tied up," and she found herself in debt for that amount. Man should receive gracefully the bread returning to him upon the water—freely ye have given, freely ye shall receive.

There is always the perfect balance of giving and receiving, and though man should give without thinking of returns, he violates law if he does not accept the returns which come to him; for all gifts are from God, man being merely the channel.

A thought of lack should never be held over the giver.

For example: When the man gave me the one cent, I did not say: "Poor man, he cannot afford to give me that." I saw him rich and prosperous, with his supply pouring in. It was this thought which brought it. If one has been a bad receiver, he must become a good one, and take even a postage stamp if it is given him, and open up his channels for receiving.

The Lord loveth a cheerful receiver, as well as a cheerful giver.

I have often been asked why one man is born rich and healthy, and another poor and sick.

Where there is an effect there is always a cause; there is no such thing as chance.

This question is answered through the law of reincarnation. Man goes through many births and deaths, until he knows the truth which sets him free.

He is drawn back to the earth plane through unsatisfied desire, to pay his Karmic debts, or to "fulfill his destiny."

The man born rich and healthy has had pictures in his subconscious mind, in his past life, of health and riches; and the poor and sick man, of disease and poverty. Man manifests, on any plane, the sum total of his subconscious beliefs.

However, birth and death are man-made laws, for the "wages of sin is death"; the Adamic fall in consciousness through the belief in two powers. The real man, spiritual man, is birthless and deathless! He never was born and has never died—"As he was in the beginning, he is now, and ever shall be!"

So through the truth, man is set free from the law of Karma, sin and death, and manifests the man made in "His image and likeness." Man's freedom comes through fulfilling his destiny, bringing into manifestation the Divine Design of his life.

His lord will say unto him: "Well done thou good and faithful servant, thou hast been faithful over a few things, I will make thee ruler over many things (death itself); enter thou into the joy of thy Lord (eternal life)."

DENIALS AND AFFIRMATIONS

"Thou shalt also decree a thing, and it shall be established unto thee."

All the good that is to be made manifest in man's life is already an accomplished fact in divine mind, and is released through man's recognition, or spoken word, so he must be careful to decree that only the Divine Idea be made manifest, for often, he decrees, through his "idle words," failure or misfortune.

It is, therefore, of the utmost importance, to word one's demands correctly, as stated in a previous chapter.

If one desires a home, friend, position or any other good thing, make the demand for the "divine selection."

For example: "Infinite Spirit, open the way for my right home, my right friend, my right position. I give thanks *it now manifests under grace in a perfect way.*"

The latter part of the statement is most important. For example: I knew a woman who demanded a thousand dollars. Her daughter was injured and they received a thousand dollars indemnity, so it did not come in a "perfect way." The demand should have been worded in this way: "Infinite Spirit, I give thanks that the one thousand dollars, which is mine by divine right, is now released, and reaches me under grace, in a perfect way."

As one grows in a financial consciousness, he should demand that the enormous sums of money, which are his by divine right, reach him under grace, in perfect ways.

It is impossible for man to release more than he thinks is possible, for one is bound by the limited expectancies of the subconscious. He must enlarge his expectancies in order to receive in a larger way.

Man so often limits himself in his demands. For example: A student made the demand for six hundred dollars, by a certain date. He did receive it, but heard afterwards, that he came very near receiving a thousand dollars, but he was given just six hundred, as the result of his spoken word.

"They limited the Holy One of Israel." Wealth is a matter of consciousness. The French have a legend giving an example of this. A poor man was walking along a road when he met a traveler, who stopped him and said: "My good friend, I see you are poor. Take this gold nugget, sell it, and you will be rich all your days."

The man was overjoyed at his good fortune, and took the nugget home. He immediately found work and became so prosperous that he did not sell the nugget. Years passed, and he became a very rich man. One day he met a poor man on the road. He stopped him and said: "My good friend, I will give you this gold nugget, which, if you sell, will make you rich for life." The mendicant took the nugget, had it valued, and found it was only brass. So we see, the first man became rich through feeling rich, thinking the nugget was gold.

CHAPTER X

Every man has within himself a gold nugget; *it is his consciousness of gold, of opulence, which brings riches into his life.* In making his demands, man begins at his *journey's end*, that is, he declares *he has already received. "Before ye call I shall answer."*

Continually affirming establishes the belief in the subconscious.

It would not be necessary to make an affirmation more than once if one had perfect faith! One should not plead or supplicate, but give thanks repeatedly, that he has received.

"The desert shall *rejoice* and blossom as the rose." This rejoicing which is yet in the desert (state of consciousness) opens the way for release. The Lord's Prayer is in the form of command and demand, "Give us this day our daily bread, and forgive us our debts as we forgive our debtors," and ends in praise, "For thine is the Kingdom and the Power and the Glory, forever. Amen." "Concerning the works of my hands, command ye me." So prayer is command and demand, praise and thanksgiving. The student's work is in making himself believe that "with God all things are possible."

This is easy enough to state in the abstract, but a little more difficult when confronted with a problem. For example: It was necessary for a woman to demonstrate a large sum of money within a stated time. She knew she must *do something* to get a realization (for realization is manifestation), and she demanded a "lead."

She was walking through a department store, when she saw a very beautiful pink enamel papercutter. She felt the "pull" towards it. The thought came. "I haven't a paper cutter good enough to open letters containing large cheques."

So she bought the papercutter, which the reasoning mind would have called an extravagance. When she held it in her hand, she had a flash of a picture of herself opening an envelope containing a large cheque, and in a few weeks, she received the money. The pink papercutter was her bridge of active faith.

Many stories are told of the power of the subconscious when directed in faith.

For example: A man was spending the night in a farm-house. The windows of the room had been nailed down, and in the middle of the night he felt suffocated and made his way in the dark to the window. He could not open it, so he smashed the pane with his fist, drew in draughts of fine fresh air, and had a wonderful night's sleep.

The next morning, he found he had smashed the glass of a bookcase and the window had remained closed during the whole night. He had *supplied himself with oxygen, simply by his thought of oxygen.*

When a student starts out to demonstrate, he should never turn back. "Let not that man who wavers think that he shall receive anything of the Lord."

A student once made this wonderful statement, "When I ask the Father for anything, I put my foot down, and I say: Father, I'll take nothing less than I've asked for, but more!" So man should never compromise: "Having done all—Stand." This is sometimes the most difficult time of demonstrating. The temptation comes to give up, to turn back, to compromise.

"He also serves who only stands and waits."

Chapter X

Demonstrations often come at the eleventh hour because man then lets go, that is, stops reasoning, and Infinite Intelligence has a chance to work.

"Man's dreary desires are answered drearily, and his impatient desires, long delayed or violently fulfilled."

For example: A woman asked me why it was she was constantly losing or breaking her glasses.

We found she often said to herself and others with vexation, "I wish I could get rid of my glasses." So her impatient desire was violently fulfilled. What she should have demanded was perfect eye-sight, but what she registered in the subconscious was simply the impatient desire to be rid of her glasses; so they were continually being broken or lost.

Two attitudes of mind cause loss: depreciation, as in the case of the woman who did not appreciate her husband, or *fear of loss*, which makes a picture of loss in the subconscious.

When a student is able to let go of his problem (cast his burden) he will have instantaneous manifestation.

For example: A woman was out during a very stormy day and her umbrella was blown inside-out. She was about to make a call on some people whom she had never met and she did not wish to make her first appearance with a dilapidated umbrella. She could not throw it away, as it did not belong to her. So in desperation, she exclaimed: "Oh, God, you take charge of this umbrella, I don't know what to do."

A moment later, a voice behind her said: "Lady, do you want your umbrella mended?" There stood an umbrella mender.

She replied, "Indeed, I do."

The man mended the umbrella, while she went into the house to pay her call, and when she returned, she had a good umbrella. So there is always an umbrella mender at hand, on man's pathway, when one puts the umbrella (or situation) in God's Hands.

One should always follow a denial with an affirmation.

For example: I was called on the 'phone late one night to treat a man whom I had never seen. He was apparently very ill. I made the statement: "I deny this appearance of disease. It is unreal, therefore cannot register in his consciousness; this man is a perfect idea in Divine Mind, pure substance expressing perfection."

There is no time or space, in Divine Mind, therefore the word reaches instantly its destination and does not "return void." I have treated patients in Europe and have found that the result was instantaneous.

I am asked so often the difference between visualizing and visioning. Visualizing is a mental process governed by the reasoning or conscious mind; visioning is a spiritual process, governed by intuition, or the superconscious mind. The student should train his mind to receive these flashes of inspiration, and work out the "divine pictures," through definite leads. When a man can say, "I desire only that which God desires for me," his false desires fade from the consciousness, and a new set of blueprints is given him by the Master Architect, the God within. God's plan for each man transcends the limitation of the reasoning mind, and is always the square of life, containing health, wealth, love and perfect self-expression. Many a man is building for himself in imagination a bungalow when he should be building a palace.

CHAPTER X

If a student tries to force a demonstration (through the reasoning mind) he brings it to a standstill. "I will hasten it," saith the Lord. He should act only through intuition, or definite leads. "Rest in the Lord and wait patiently. Trust also in him, and he will bring it to pass."

I have seen the law work in the most astonishing manner. For example: A student stated that it was necessary for her to have a hundred dollars by the following day. It was a debt of vital importance which had to be met. I "spoke the word," declaring Spirit was "never too late" and that the supply was at hand.

That evening she 'phoned me of the miracle. She said that the thought came to her to go to her safety-deposit box at the bank to examine some papers. She looked over the papers, and at the bottom of the box, was a new one hundred dollar-bill. She was astounded, and said she knew she had never put it there, for she had gone through the papers many times. It may have been a materialization, as Jesus Christ materialized the loaves and fishes. Man will reach the stage where his "word is made flesh," or materialized, instantly. "The fields, ripe with the harvest," will manifest immediately, as in all of the miracles of Jesus Christ.

There is a tremendous power alone in the name Jesus Christ. It stands for *Truth Made Manifest*. He said, "Whatsoever ye ask the Father, in y name, he will give it to you."

The power of this name raises the student into the fourth dimension, where he is freed from all astral and psychic influences, and he becomes "unconditioned and absolute, as God Himself is unconditioned and absolute."

I have seen many healings accomplished by using the words, "In the name of Jesus Christ."

Christ was both person and principle; and the Christ within each man is his Redeemer and Salvation.

The Christ within, is his own fourth dimensional self, the man made in God's image and likeness. This is the self which has never failed, never known sickness or sorrow, was never born and has never died. It is the "resurrection and the life" of each man! "No man cometh to the Father save by the Son," means, that God, the Universal, working on the place of the particular, becomes the Christ in man; and the Holy Ghost, means God-inaction. So daily, man is manifesting the Trinity of Father, Son and Holy Ghost.

Man should make an art of thinking. The Master Thinker is an artist and is careful to paint only the divine designs upon the canvas of his mind; and he paints these pictures with masterly strokes of power and decision, having perfect faith that there is no power to mar their perfection and that they shall manifest in his life the ideal made real.

All power is given man (through right thinking) to bring *his heaven* upon *his earth*, and this is the *goal of the "Game of Life."*

The simple rules are fearless faith, nonresistance and love!

May each reader be now freed from that thing which has held him in bondage through the ages, standing between him and his own, and "know the Truth which makes him free"—free to fulfill his destiny, to bring into manifestation the *"Divine Design of his life*, Health, Wealth, Love and Perfect Self-Expression." "Be ye transformed by the renewing of your mind."

90

Denials and Affirmations

(For Prosperity)

God is my unfailing supply, and large sums of money come to me quickly, under grace, in perfect ways.

(For Right Conditions)

Every plan my Father in heaven has not planned, shall be dissolved and dissipated, and the Divine Idea now comes to pass.

(For Right Conditions)

Only that which is true of God is true of me, for I and the Father are ONE.

(For Faith)

As I am one with God, I am one with my good, for God is both the *Giver* and the *Gift*. I cannot separate the *Giver* from the gift.

(For Right Conditions)

Divine Love now dissolves and dissipates every wrong condition in my mind, body and affairs. Divine Love is the most powerful chemical in the universe, and *dissolves everything* which is not of itself!

(For Health)

Divine Love floods my consciousness with health, and every cell in my body is filled with light.

(For the Eyesight)

My eyes are God's eyes, I see with the eyes of spirit. I see clearly the open way; there are no obstacles on my pathway. I see clearly the perfect plan.

(For Guidance)

I am divinely sensitive to my intuitive leads, and give instant obedience to Thy will.

(For the Hearing)

My ears are God's ears, I hear with the ears of spirit. I am nonresistant and am willing to be led. I hear glad tidings of great joy.

(For Right Work)

I have a perfect work
In a perfect way;
I give a perfect service
For perfect pay.

(For Freedom from all Bondage)

I cast this burden on the Christ within, and I go free!

THE SECRET DOOR TO SUCCESS

CONTENTS

THE SECRET DOOR
TO SUCCESS

"So the people shouted when the priests blew with the trumpets: and it came to pass, when the people heard the sound of the trumpet, and the people shouted with a great shout, that the wall fell down flat, so that the people went up into the city, every man straight before him, and they took the city."—Joshua 6:20

A successful man is always asked—"What is the secret of your success?"

People never ask a man who is a failure, "What is the secret of your failure?" It is quite easy to see and they are not interested.

People all want to know how to open the secret door of success.

For each man there is success, but it seems to be behind a door or wall. In the Bible reading, we have heard the wonderful story of the falling of the walls of Jericho.

Of course all biblical stories have a metaphysical interpretation.

We will talk now about *your* wall of Jericho: the wall separating *you* from *success*. Nearly everyone has built a wall around his own Jericho.

This city you are not able to enter, contains great treasures; your divinely designed success, your heart's desire!

What kind of wall have you built around your Jericho? Often, it is a wall of resentment—resenting someone, or resenting a situation, shuts off your good.

If you are a failure and resent the success of someone else, you are keeping away your own success.

I have given the following statement to neutralize envy and resentment.

What God has done for others, He now does for me and more.

A woman was filled with envy because a friend had received a gift, she made this statement, and an exact duplicate of the gift was given her—plus another present.

It was when the children of Israel shouted, that the walls of Jericho fell down. When you make an affirmation of Truth, your wall of Jericho totters.

I gave the following statement to a woman: *The walls of lack and delay now crumble away, and I enter my Promised Land, under grace.* She had a vivid picture of stepping over a fallen wall, and received the demonstration of her good, almost immediately.

It is the word of realization which brings about a change in your affairs; for words and thoughts are a form of radio-activity.

Taking an interest in your work, enjoying what you are doing opens the secret door to success.

A number of years ago I went to California to speak at the different centers, by way of the Panama Canal, and on the boat I met a man named Jim Tully.

For years he had been a tramp. He called himself The King of the Hoboes.

CHAPTER XI

He was ambitious and picked up an education.

He had a vivid imagination and commenced writing stories about his experiences.

He dramatized tramp life, he enjoyed what he was doing, and became a very successful author. I remember one book called "Outside Looking In." It was made into a motion picture.

He is now famous and prosperous and lives in Hollywood. What opened the secret door to success for Jim Tully?

Dramatizing his life—being interested in what he was doing, he made the most of being a tramp. On the boat, we all sat at the captain's table, which gave us a chance to talk.

Mrs. Grace Stone was also a passenger on the boat; she had written the "Bitter Tea of General Yen," and was going to Hollywood to have it made into a moving-picture: she had lived in China and was inspired to write the book.

That is the *Secret* of Success, to *make what you are doing interesting to other people.* Be interested yourself, and others will find you interesting.

A good disposition, a smile, often opens the secret door; the Chinese say, "A man without a smiling face, must not open a shop."

The success of a smile was brought out in a French moving-picture in which Chevalier took the lead, the picture was called, "With a Smile." One of the characters had become poor, dreary and almost a derelict; He said to Chevalier "What good has my honesty done me?" Chevalier replied, "Even honesty won't help you, without a smile:" so the man changes on the spot, cheers up, and becomes very successful.

Living in the past, complaining of your misfortunes, builds a thick wall around your Jericho.

Talking too much about your affairs, scattering your forces, brings you up against a high wall. I knew a man of brains and ability, who was a complete failure.

He lived with his mother and aunt, and I found that every night when he went home to dinner, he told them all that had taken place during the day at the office; he discussed his hopes, his fears, and his failures.

I said to him, "You scatter your forces by talking about your affairs. Don't discuss your business with your family. Silence is Golden!"

He took my lead. During dinner he refused to talk about business, His mother and aunt were in despair: They loved to hear all about everything; but his silence proved golden!

Not long after, he was given a position at one hundred dollars a week, and in a few years, he had a salary of three hundred dollars a week.

Success is not a secret, it is a System.

Many people are up against the wall of discouragement. Courage and endurance are part of the system. We read this in lives of all successful men and women.

I had an amusing experience which brought this to my notice. I went to a moving picture theatre to meet a friend.

While waiting, I stood near a young boy, selling programs.

He called to people passing, "Buy a complete program of the picture, containing photographs of the actors and a sketch of their lives."

Most people passed by without buying. To my great surprise, he suddenly turned to me, and said—"Say, this ain't no racket for a guy with ambition!"

Then he gave a discourse on success. He said, "Most people give up just before something big is coming to them. A successful man never gives up.

Of course I was interested and said, "I'll bring you a book the next time I come. It is called *The Game of Life and How to Play It.* You will agree with a lot of the ideas."

A week or two later I went back with the book.

The girl at the ticket office said to him—"Let me read it, Eddie, while you are selling programs." The man who took tickets leaned over to see what it was about.

"The Game of Life" always gets people's interest.

I returned to the theatre in about three weeks, Eddie had gone. He had expanded into a new job that he liked. His wall of Jericho had crumbled, he had refused to be discouraged.

Only twice, is the word *success* mentioned in the Bible— both times in the Book of Joshua.

"Only be strong and very courageous to observe to do according to all the law which Moses, my servant, commanded thee: turn not from it to the right nor to the left, that thou mayest have good success whithersoever thou goest. This book of the law shall not depart from thy mouth, but thou shalt meditate therein day and night, that thou mayest observe to do all that is written therein, for then shalt thou make thy way prosperous and thou shalt have good success. Turn not to the right nor to the left."

The *road to success* is a *straight and narrow path; it is a road of loving absorption, of undivided attention.*

"You attract the things you give a great deal of thought to."

So if you give a great deal of thought to lack, you attract lack, if you give a great deal of thought to injustice, you attract more injustice.

Joshua said, "And it shall come to pass, that when they make a long blast with the ram's horn, and when ye hear the sound of the trumpet, all the people shall shout with a great shout: and the wall of the city shall fall down flat, and the people shall ascend up, every man straight before him."

The inner meaning of this story, is the power of the word, your word which dissolves obstacles, and removes barriers.

When the people shouted the walls fell down.

We find in folk-lore and fairy stories, which come down from legends founded on Truth, the same idea—a word opens a door or cleaves a rock.

We have it again in the Arabian Night's Story, "Ali Baba and The Forty Thieves." I saw it made into a moving picture.

Ali Baba has a secret hiding place, hidden somewhere behind rocks and mountains, the entrance may only be gained by speaking a secret word.—It is "Open Sesame!"

Ali Baba faces the mountain and cries—"Open Sesame!" and the rocks slide apart.

It is very inspiring, for it gives you the realization of how YOUR own rocks and barriers, *will part at the right word.*

> So let us now take the statement—The walls of lack and delay now crumble away, and I enter my Promised Land, under grace.

BRICKS WITHOUT STRAW

"There shall no straw be given you, yet ye shall make bricks without straw."—Exodus 5:18

In the 5th chapter of Exodus, we have a picture of every day life, when giving a metaphysical interpretation.

The Children of Israel were in bondage to Pharaoh, the cruel taskmaster, ruler of Egypt. They were kept in slavery, making bricks, and were hated and despised.

Moses had orders from the Lord to deliver his people from bondage—"Moses and Aaron went in and told Pharaoh—Thus saith the Lord God of Israel, Let my people go, that they may hold a feast unto me in the wilderness."

He not only refused to let them go, but told them he would make their tasks even more difficult: they must make bricks without straw being provided for them.

"And the task-masters of the people went out, and their officers, and they spake to the people, saying, Thus saith Pharaoh, I will not give you straw."

"Go ye, get you straw where ye can find it: yet not ought of your work shall be diminished."

It was impossible to make bricks without straw. The Children of Israel were completely crushed by Pharaoh, they were beaten for not producing the bricks—Then came the message from Jehovah.

"Go therefore now, and work; for there shall no straw be given you, yet shall ye deliver the tale (number) of bricks."

Working with Spiritual law they could make bricks without straw, which means to accomplish the seemingly impossible.

How often in life people are confronted with this situation.

Agnes M. Lawson in her "Hints to Bible Students" says— "The Life in Egypt under foreign oppression is the symbol of man under the hard taskmasters of Destructive thinking, Pride, Fear, Resentment, Ill-will, etc. The deliverance under Moses is the freedom man gains from the taskmasters, as he learns the law of life, for we can never come under grace, except we first know the law. The law must be made known in order to be fulfilled."

In the 111th Psalm we read in the final verse, "The fear of the Lord (law) is the beginning of Wisdom: a good understanding have all they that do his commandments: his praise endureth forever."

Now if we read the word Lord (law) it will give us the key to the statement.

The fear of the law (Karmic law) is the beginning of wisdom (not the fear of the Lord).

When we know that whatever we send out comes back, we begin to be afraid of our own boomerangs.

I read in a medical journal the following facts telling of the Boomerang this great Pharaoh received.

"It would appear that flesh is indeed heir to a long and ancient line of ills, when, as was revealed by Lord Monyahan at a lecture at Leeds, that the Pharaoh of the oppression suffered from hardening of the heart in a literal sense; Lord Monyahan showed some remarkable photographic slides of results of surgical operations a thousand years before Christ, and among these was a slide of the actual anatomical remains of the Pharaoh of the Oppression.

"The large vessel springing from the heart was in such a well-preserved state, as to enable sections of it to be made and compared with those made recently from the lantern slide. It was impossible to distinguish between the ancient and modern vessel. Both hearts had been attacked by Atheroma, a condition in which calcium salts are deposited in the walls of the vessel, making it rigid and inelastic.

"Inadequate expanse to the stream of blood from the heart caused the vessel to give way; with this condition went the mental changes that occur with a rigid arterial system: *A narrowness of outlook; restriction and dread of enterprise, a literal hardening of the heart.*"

So Pharaoh's hardness of heart, hardened his own heart.

This is as true today as it was several thousand years ago—we are all coming out of the Land of Egypt, out of the House of Bondage.

Your doubts and fears keep you in slavery; you face a situation which seems hopeless; What can you do? It is a case of making bricks without straw.

But remember the words of Jehovah, "Go therefore now, and work; for there shall no straw be given you, yet shall ye deliver the tale (number) of bricks."

You shall make bricks without straw. God makes a way where there is no way!

I was told the story of a woman who needed money for her rent: it was necessary to have it at once, she knew of no channel, she had exhausted every avenue.

However, she was a Truth student, and kept making her affirmations. Her dog whined and wanted to go out, she put on his leash and walked down the street, in the accustomed direction.

However, the dog pulled at his leash and wanted to go in another direction.

She followed, and in the middle of the block, opposite an open park, she looked down, and picked up a roll of bills, which exactly covered her rent.

She looked for ads, but never found the owner. There were no houses near where she found it.

The reasoning mind, the intellect, takes the throne of Pharaoh in your consciousness. It says continually, "It can't be done. What's the use!"

We must drown out these dreary suggestions with a vital affirmation!

For example take this statement: "*The unexpected happens, my seemingly impossible good now comes to pass.*" This stops all argument from the army of the aliens (the reasoning mind).

"The unexpected happens!" That is an idea it cannot cope with.

"Thou hast made me wiser than mine enemies." Your enemy thoughts, your doubts, fears and apprehensions!

Think of the joy of really being free forever, from the Pharaoh of the oppression. To have the idea of *security, health, happiness and abundance established in the subconscious.* It would mean a life free from all limitation!

CHAPTER XII

It would be the Kingdom which Jesus Christ spoke of, where all things are automatically added unto us. I say automatically added unto us, because all life is vibration; and when we vibrate to success, happiness and abundance, the things which symbolize these states of consciousness will attach themselves to us.

Feel rich and successful, and suddenly you receive a large cheque or a beautiful gift.

I tell the story showing the working of this law. I went to a party where people played games, and whoever won, received a gift. The prize was a beautiful fan.

Among those present, was a very rich woman, who had everything. Her name was Clara. The poorer and resentful ones got together and whispered: "We hope Clara doesn't get the fan." Of course Clara won the fan.

She was care-free and vibrating to abundance. *Envy and resentment short-circuit your good* and keep away your fans.

If you should happen to be resentful and envious, take the statement; *What God has done for others He now does for me and more!*

Then all the fans and things will come your way.

No man gives to himself but himself, and no man takes away from himself but himself: the "Game of Life" is a game of solitaire; as you change, all conditions will change.

Now to go back to Pharaoh the oppressor; no one loves an oppressor.

I remember a friend I had many years ago, her name was Lettie; her father had plenty of money and supplied her mother and herself with food and clothes, but no luxuries.

We went to Art School together, and all the students would buy reproductions of the "Winged Victory," "Whistler's Mother" or something to bring art into their homes.

My friend's father called all these things "plunder." He would say, "Don't bring home any plunder."

So she lived a colorless life without a "Winged Victory" on her bureau or "Whistler's Mother" on the wall.

He would say often to my friend and her mother, "When I die, you'll both be well off."

One day someone said to Lettie, "When are you going abroad?" (all art students went abroad.)

She replied, cheerfully, "Not 'till Papa dies."

So people always look forward to being free from lack and oppression.

Let us now free ourselves from the *tyrants of negative thinking:* we have been slaves to doubts, fears and apprehension and let us be delivered as Moses delivered the Children of Israel; and come out of the Land of Egypt, out of the House of Bondage.

Find the thought which is your great oppressor; find the *King-Pin.*

In the logging camps in the Spring, the logs are sent down the rivers in great numbers.

Sometimes the logs become crossed and cause a jam; the men look for the log causing the jam (they call it the King-Pin), straighten it, and the logs rush down the river again.

Maybe your King-Pin is resentment, resentment holds back your good.

Chapter XII

The more you resent, the more you will have to resent; you grow a resentment track in your brain, and your expression will be one of habitual resentment.

You will be avoided and miss the golden opportunities which await you each day.

I remember a few years ago, the streets were filled with men selling apples.

They got up early to get the good corners.

I passed one several times on Park Avenue, he had the most disagreeable expression I have ever seen.

As people passed he said, "Apples! Apples!" but no one stopped to buy.

I invested in an apple and said, "You'll never sell apples unless you change your expression."

He replied, "Well that guy over there took my corner."

I said, "Never mind about the corner, you can sell apples right here if you'll look pleasant."

He said "O.K. lady," and I went on. The next day I saw him, his whole expression had changed; he was doing a big business, selling apples with a smile.

So find your King-Pin—(you may have more than one); and your logs of *success, happiness and abundance will go rushing down your river.*

"Go therefore now and work, for there shall no straw be given you, yet ye shall make bricks without out straw."

XIII

"AND FIVE OF THEM WERE WISE"

"And five of them were wise, and five were foolish. They that were foolish took their lamps, and took no oil with them."—Matt. 25:2:3

My subject is the parable of the Wise and the Foolish Virgins. "And five of them were wise, and five were foolish. They that were foolish took their lamps, and took no oil with them. But the wise took oil in their vessels with their lamps." The parable teaches that true prayer means preparation.

Jesus Christ said, "And all things, whatsoever ye shall ask in prayer, *believing*, ye shall receive" (Math. 21:22). "Therefore I say unto you, what things soever ye desire, when ye pray, believe that ye receive them, and ye shall have them" (Mark 11:24). In this parable he shows that only those who have prepared for their good (thereby showing active faith) will bring the manifestation to pass.

We might paraphrase the scriptures and say: When ye pray believe ye have it. When ye pray ACT as if you have already received.

Armchair faith or rocking chair faith, will never move mountains. In the armchair, in the silence, or meditation, you are filled

111

with the wonder of this Truth, and feel that your faith will never waver. You know that The Lord is your Shepherd, you shall never want.

You feel that your God of Plenty will wipe out all burdens of debt or limitations. Then you leave your armchair and step out into the arena of Life. It is only what you do in the arena that counts.

I will give you an illustration showing how the law works; for faith without action is dead.

A man, one of my students, had a great desire to go abroad. He took the statement: *I give thanks for my divinely designed trip, divinely financed, under grace, in a perfect way.* He had very little money, but knowing the law of preparation, he bought a trunk. It was a very gay and happy trunk with a big red band around its waist. Whenever he looked at it it gave him a realization of a trip. One day he seemed to feel his room moving. He felt the motion of a ship. He went to the window to breathe the fresh air, and it smelt like the aroma of the docks. With his inner ear he heard the shriek of a sea-gull and the creaking of the gangplank. The trunk had commenced to work. It had put him in the vibration of his trip. Soon after that, a large sum of money came to him and he took the trip. He said afterwards that it was perfect in every detail.

In the arena of Life we must keep ourselves tuned-up to concert pitch.

Are we acting from motives of fear or faith? *Watch your motives with all diligence, for out of them are the issues of life.*

If your problem is a financial one (and it usually is), you must know how to wind yourself up financially, and keep wound up by always acting your faith. The material attitude towards money is to trust in your salary, your income and investments, which can shrink over night.

The spiritual attitude toward money is to trust in God for your supply. To keep your possessions, always realize that they are God in manifestation. "What Allah has given cannot be diminished," then if one door shuts another door, immediately, opens.

Never voice lack or limitation for "by your words you are condemned." You combine with what you notice, and if you are always noticing failure and hard times, you will combine with failure and hard times.

You must form the habit of living in the fourth dimension, "The World of the Wondrous." It is the world where you do not judge by appearances.

You have trained your inner eye to see through failure into success, to see through sickness into health to see through limitation into plenty. I will give you the land which your inner eye sees. "I will give to you the land which thou seeth."

The man who achieves success has the *fixed idea of success.* If it is founded on a rock of truth and rightness it will stand. If not, it is built upon sand and washed into the sea, returning to its native nothingness.

Only divine ideas can endure. Evil destroys itself, for it is a cross current against universal order, and the way of the transgressor is hard.

"They that were foolish took their lamps, and took no oil with them. But the wise took oil in their vessels with their lamps."

The lamp symbolizes man's consciousness. The oil is what brings Light or understanding.

"While the bridegroom tarried, they all slumbered and slept. And at midnight there was a cry made, Behold, the bridegroom cometh; go ye out to meet him. Then all those virgins arose, and trimmed their lamps. And the foolish said unto the wise, Give us your oil; for our lamps are gone out."

The foolish virgins were without wisdom or understanding, which is oil for the consciousness, and when they were confronted with a serious situation, they had no way of handling it.

And when they said to the wise "give us of your oil," the wise answered saying, "Not so; lest there be not enough for us and you: but go ye rather to them that sell, and buy for yourselves."

That means that the foolish virgins could *not receive more than was in their consciousness,* or what they were vibrating to.

The man received the trip because it was in his consciousness, as a reality. He believed that he had already received. As he prepared for the trip he was taking oil for his lamps. With *realization comes manifestation.*

The law of preparation works both ways. If you prepare for what you fear or don't want, you begin to attract it. David said, "The thing I feared has come upon me." We hear people say, "I must put away money in case of illness." They are deliberately preparing to be ill. Or, "I'm saving for a rainy day." The rainy day is sure to come, at a most inconvenient time.

The divine idea for every man is plenty. Your barns *should be* full, and your cup *should* flow over, but we must learn to ask aright.

For example take this statement: *I call on the law of accumulation. My supply comes from God, and now pours in and piles up, under grace.*

This statement does not give any picture of stint or saving or sickness. It gives a fourth dimensional feeling of abundance, leaving the channels to Infinite Intelligence.

Every day you must make a choice, will you be wise or foolish? Will you prepare for your good? Will you *take the giant swing into faith*? Or serve doubt and fear and bring no oil for your lamps?

"And while they went to buy, the bridegroom came; and they that were ready went in with him to the marriage: and the door was shut. Afterward came also the other virgins, saying, Lord, Lord, open to us. But he answered and said, Verily I say unto you, I know you not."

You may feel that the foolish virgins paid very dearly for neglecting to bring oil for their lamps, but we are dealing with the law of Karma (or the law of come back). It has been called the "judgement day," which people usually associate with the end of the world.

Your judgement day comes, they say, in sevens—seven hours, seven days, seven weeks, seven months, or seven years. It might even come in seven minutes. Then you pay some Karmic debt; the price for having violated spiritual law. *You failed to trust God, you took no oil for your lamps.*

Every day examine your consciousness and see just what you are preparing for. You are fearful of lack and hang on to every cent, thereby attracting more lack. Use what you have with wisdom and it opens the way for more to come to you.

In my book, "Your Word Is Your Wand," I tell about the Magic Purse. In the Arabian Nights they tell the story of a man who had a Magic Purse. As money went out, immediately money appeared in it again.

So I made the statement: *My supply comes from God—I have the magic purse of the spirit. It can never be depleted. As money goes out, immediately money comes in. It is always crammed, jammed with abundance, under grace, in perfect ways.*

This brings a vivid picture to mind: You are drawing on the bank of the imagination.

A woman who did not have much money was afraid to pay any bills and see her bank account dwindle. It came to her with great conviction: "I have the magic purse of the spirit. It can never be depleted. As money goes out, immediately, money comes in." She fearlessly paid her bills, and several large cheques came to her that she did not expect.

"Watch and pray lest ye enter into the temptation" of preparing for something destructive instead of something constructive.

I knew a woman who told me she always kept a long crepe veil handy in case of funerals. I said to her, "You are a menace to your relatives, and are preparing to hurry them all off, so that you can wear the veil." She destroyed it.

Another woman who had no money decided to send her two daughters to college. Her husband scorned the idea and said, "Who will pay their tuition? I have no money for it." She replied, "I know some *unforeseen good will come to us.*" She kept on preparing her daughters for college. Her husband laughed heartily and told all their friends that his wife was sending the girls to college on "some unforeseen good." A rich relative suddenly sent her a large sum of money. "Some unforeseen good" *did* arrive, for she had shown active faith. I asked what she had said to her husband when the cheque arrived. She replied, "Oh, I never antagonize George by telling him I am in the right."

So prepare for your "unforeseen good." Let every thought and every act express your unwavering faith. Every event in your life is a crystallized idea. Something you have invited through either fear or faith. *Something you have prepared for.*

So let us be wise and bring oil for our lamps—and when we least expect it, we shall reap the fruits of our faith.

> My lamps are now filled with the oil of faith and fulfillment.

XIV

WHAT DO YOU EXPECT?

"According to your faith be it unto you."—Matt. 9:29

Faith is expectancy, "According to your faith, be it unto you."

We might say, according to your expectancies be it done unto you; so, what are you expecting?

We hear people say: "We expect the worst to happen," or "The worst is yet to come." They are deliberately inviting the worst to come.

We hear others say: "I expect a change for the better." They are inviting better conditions into their lives.

Change your expectancies and you change your conditions.

How can you change your expectancies, when you have formed the habit of expecting loss, lack or failure?

Begin to act as if you *expected* success, happiness and abundance; *prepare for your good.*

Do something to show you expect it to come. Active faith alone, will impress the subconscious.

If you have spoken the word for a home, prepare for it immediately, as if you hadn't a moment to lose. Collect little ornaments, table-cloths, etc. etc.!

I knew a woman who made the giant swing into faith, by buying a large arm-chair; a chair meant business, she bought a large and comfortable chair, for she was preparing for the right man. He came.

Someone will say, "Suppose you haven't money to buy ornaments or a chair?" Then look in shop windows and link with them in thought.

Get in their vibration: I sometimes hear people say; "I don't go into the shops because I can't afford to buy anything." That is just the reason you should go into the shops. Begin to make friends with the things you desire or require.

I know a woman who wanted a ring. She went boldly to the ring department and tried on rings.

It gave her such a realization of ownership, that not long after, a friend made her a gift of a ring. "You combine with what you notice."

Keep on noticing beautiful things, and you make an invisible contact. Sooner or later these things are drawn into your life, unless you say, "Poor me, too good to be true."

"My soul, wait thou only upon God: for my expectation is from Him." This is a most important statement from the 62nd Psalm.

The soul is the subconscious mind, and the psalmist was telling his subconscious to expect everything directly from the universal; not to depend upon doors and channels; "My expectation is from Him."

God cannot fail, for "His ways are ingenious, His methods are sure."

You can expect any seemingly impossible Good from God; if you do not limit the channels.

Do not say how you want it done, or how it can't be done.

"God is the Giver and the Gift *and creates His own amazing channels.*"

Take the following statement: *I cannot be separated from God the Giver, therefore, I cannot be separated from God the Gift. The gift is God in action.*

Get the realization that every blessing is *Good in action,* and see God in every face and good in every situation: This makes you master of all conditions.

A woman came to me saying that there was no heat in the radiators in their apartment, and that her mother was suffering from the cold. She added, "The landlord has declared that we can't have heat until a certain date:" I replied, "God is your landlord." She said, "That's all I want to know," and rushed out. That evening the heat was turned on without asking. It was because she realized that the landlord was God in manifestation.

This is a wonderful age, for people are becoming Miracle Minded; it is in the air.

Quoting from an article which I found in the New York Journal and American by John Anderson, it corroborates what I have just said.

The title of the article is "Theatre Goers Make Hits of Metaphysical Plays."

If, said a cynical manager, who shall be called Brock Pemberton, with a slight accent of sarcasm in his voice, the other night, on an intermission curbside talk, you fellows, meaning the critics, know so much about what the New York public wants, why don't you tell me what to produce? Why don't you run me into business instead of out of it? "Why don't you tell me what sort of play the play-goers want to see?" "I would," I said, "But you wouldn't believe it."

"You're hedging," he said, "You don't know, and you're trying to cover up by pretending to know more than you're willing to say. You haven't any more idea than I have this minute what sort of plays generally succeed."

"I have," I said, "there is one sure fire success; one theme that works and has always worked, whether it is competing with boy meets girl, mysteries, historical tragedies, etc.; no play on the theme has ever completely failed if it had any merit at all, and a lot of poor ones have been big hits."

"You're stalling again," said Mr. Pemberton, "What sort of plays are they?"

"Metaphysical," I said, fouling slightly with a big word and waiting quietly for the effect. "Metaphysical," said Mr. Pemberton, "You mean metaphysical?"

I paused a moment and since Mr. Pemberton said nothing, went right on spouting such titles as "The Green Pastures," "The Star Wagon," "Father Malachy's Miracle!, etc." "Some of these," I added, "reached the public *over* the heads of the critics." But Mr. Pemberton had departed to ask probably, in every theatre in town, "Is there a metaphysician in the house?"

People are beginning to realize the power of their words and thoughts. They understand why "Faith *is* the substance of the thing hoped for, the evidence of things not seen."

We see the law of expectancy working out through superstition.

If you walk under a ladder and expect it to give you bad luck, it will give you bad luck. The ladder is quite innocent; bad luck came because you expected it.

CHAPTER XIV

We might say, expectancy is the substance of the things hoped for; or expectancy is the substance of the thing man fears; "The thing I expected has come upon me."

Nothing as too good to be true, nothing is too wonderful to happen, nothing is too good to last; when you look to God for your good.

Now think of the blessings which seem so far off, and begin to expect them now, under grace, in an unexpected way; for God works in unexpected ways, His wonders to perform.

I was told that there are three thousand promises in the Bible.

Let us now expect all these blessings to come to pass. Among them we are promised Riches and Honor, Eternal Youth ("Your flesh shall become as a little child's") and Eternal Life, "death itself shall be overcome."

Christianity as founded upon the forgiveness of sins and an empty tomb.

We now know that all these things are scientifically possible.

As we call on the law of forgiveness, we become free from mistakes and the consequences of mistakes. ("Though your sins be as scarlet ye shall be washed whiter than wool.")

Then our bodies will be bathed in Light, and express the "body electric," which is incorruptible and indestructible, pure substance, expressing perfection.

I expect the unexpected, my glorious good now comes to pass.

XV

THE LONG ARM OF GOD

"The Eternal God is thy refuge, and underneath are the everlasting arms."—Deut. 33:27

In the bible, the arm of God always symbolizes protection. The writers of the bible knew the power of a symbol. It brings a picture which impresses the subconscious mind. They used the symbols of the rock, sheep, shepherds, vineyard, lamp, and hundreds of others. It would be interesting to know how many symbols are used in the bible. The arm also symbolizes strength.

"The eternal God is thy refuge, and underneath are the everlasting arms: and he shall thrust out the enemy from before thee; and shall say, Destroy them."

Who is the enemy "before thee." The negative thought-forms which you have built up in your subconscious mind. A man's enemies are only those of his own household. The everlasting arms thrust out these enemy thoughts and destroy them.

Have you ever felt the relief of getting out some negative thought-form? Perhaps you have built up a thought-form of resentment, until you are always boiling with anger about something. You resent people you know, people you don't know—people in the past and people in the present; and you may be sure that the people in the future won't escape your wrath.

All the organs of the body are affected by resentment—for when you resent, you resent with every organ of the body. You pay the penalty with rheumatism, arthritis, neuritis, etc., for acid thoughts produce acid in the blood. All this trouble comes because you are fighting the battle, not leaving it to the long arm of God.

I have given the following statement to many of my students. *The long arm of God reaches out over people and conditions, controlling this situation and protecting my interests.*

This brings a picture of a long arm symbolizing strength and protection. With the realization of the power of the long arm of God, you would no longer resist or resent. You would relax and let go. The enemy thoughts within you would be destroyed, therefore, *the adverse conditions would disappear.*

Spiritual development means the ability to stand still, or stand aside, and let Infinite Intelligence lift your burdens and fight your battles. When the burden of resentment is lifted, you experience a sense of relief! You have a kindly feeling for everyone, and all the organs of your body begin to function properly.

A clipping quoting Albert Edward Day, D.D. reads, "That loving our enemies is good for our spiritual health is widely known and accepted. But that negation and poisonous emotions destroy physical health, is a relatively new discovery. The problem of health is often an emotional one. Wrong emotions entertained and repeated are potent causes of illness. When the preacher talks about loving your enemies, the man on the street is apt to dismiss the idea as unendurable and pious. But the fact is, the preacher is telling you something which is one of the first laws of hygiene, as well as ethics. No man even for his body's sake can afford to indulge in hatred. It is like repeated doses of poison. When you are urged to get rid of fear, you are not listening to a moon-struck idealist; rather you are hearing counsel that is as significant for health as advice about diet."

We hear so much about a balanced diet, but without a balanced mind you can't digest what you eat, calories or no calories.

Non-resistance is an art. When acquired, The World is Yours! So many people are trying to force situations. Your lasting good will never come through forcing personal will.

> "Flee from the things which flee from thee,
> Seek nothing, fortune seeketh thee.
> Behold his shadow on the floor!
> Behold him standing at the door!"

I do not know the author of these lines. Lovelock, the celebrated English athlete, was asked how to attain his speed and endurance in running. He replied, "Learn to relax." Let us attain this rest in action. He was most relaxed when running the fastest.

Your big opportunity and big success usually *slide in*, when you least expect it. You have to let go long enough for the *great law of attraction to operate. You never saw a worried and anxious magnet.* It stands up straight and hasn't a care in the world, because it knows the needles can't help jumping to it. The things we rightly desire come to pass when we have taken the clutch off.

I say in my correspondence course, "*Do not let your heart's desire become a heart's disease.*" *You are completely demagnetized when you desire something too intensely.* You worry, fear, and agonize. There is an occult law of indifference: "None of these things move me." *Your ships come in over a don't care sea.*

Many people in Truth antagonize friends, because they are too anxious for them to read the books and go to the lectures. They meet opposition.

A friend took my book, "The Game of Life and How to Play It" to her brother's house to read. The young men of the family refused to read it. No "nut stuff" for them. One of these young men drives a taxi cab. One night he drove a taxi which belonged to another man. In going over the car he found a book stuffed away somewhere. It was "The Game of Life and How to Play It." The next day he said to his aunt, "I found Mrs. Shinn's book in the taxi last night. I read it and it's great! There's a lot of good reading in it. Why doesn't she write another book?" God works in roundabout ways, His wonders to perform.

I meet unhappy people and a few grateful and contented people. A man said to me one day, "I have a great deal to be thankful for. I have good health, enough money and I'm still single!"

The eighty-ninth psalm is very interesting, for we find that two individuals take part; the man who sings the psalm (for all psalms are songs or poems), and the Lord God of Hosts answers him. It is a song of praise and thanksgiving, extolling the strong arm of God.

"I will sing of the mercies of the Lord forever!"

"O Lord God of Hosts, who is a strong Lord like unto thee?"

"Thou hast a mighty arm: strong is thy hand, and high is thy right hand."

Then the Lord of Hosts replies.

"With whom my hand shall be established: mine arm also shall strengthen him."

"My mercy will I keep for him for evermore, and my covenant shall stand fast with him."

We only hear the words "for evermore" in the bible and in fairy-tales. In the absolute, man is outside of time and space. His good is "from everlasting to everlasting." The fairy-tales came down from the old Persian legends which were founded upon Truth.

Aladdin and His Wonderful Lamp is the out-picturing of the Word. Aladdin rubbed the lamp and all his desires came to pass. Your word is your lamp. Words and thoughts are a form of radio activity and do not return void. A scientist has said that words are clothed in light. *You are continually reaping the fruits of your words.*

A friend in one of my meeting said that she had brought a man to my class who had been out of work for a year or more. I gave the statement: *Now is the appointed time. Today is the day of my amazing good fortune.* It clicked in his consciousness. Soon after, he was given a position which paid him nine thousand dollars a year.

A woman told me that when I blessed the offering I said that each offering would return a thousandfold. She had put a dollar in the collection. She said with great realization, "That dollar is blessed and returns a thousand dollars." She received a thousand dollars a short time afterwards, in a most unexpected way.

Why do some people demonstrate this Truth so much more quickly than others? It is because they have the ears that hear. Jesus Christ tells the parable of the man who sowed the seed and it fell upon good ground. The seed is the word. I say, *"Listen for the statement that clicks; the statement that gives you realization. That statement will bear fruit."*

The other day I went into a shop where I know the employer quite well. I had given one of his employees an affirmation card. I said to him, jokingly, "I wouldn't waste an affirmation card on you. You wouldn't use it." He replied, "Oh, sure, give me one. I'll use it." The following week I gave him a card. Before I left he rushed up to me excitedly and said, "I made that statement and two new customers walked in." It was: "Now is the appointed time; today is the day of my amazing good fortune." It had clicked.

So many people use their words in exaggerated and reckless statements. I find a great deal of material for my talks in the beauty parlor. A young girl wanted a magazine to read. She called to the operator, "Give me something terribly new and frightfully exciting." All she wanted was the latest moving picture magazine. You hear people say, "I wish something terribly exciting would happen." They are inviting some unhappy, but exciting, experience into their lives. Then they wonder why it happened to them.

There should be a chair of metaphysics in all colleges. *Metaphysics is the wisdom of the ages.* It is the ancient wisdom taught all through the centuries in India and Egypt and

Greece. Hermes Trismegistus was a great teacher of Egypt. His teachings were closely guarded and have come down to us over ten centuries. He lived in Egypt in the days when the present race of men was in its infancy. But if you read the "Kybalion" carefully, you will find that he taught just what we are teaching today. He said that all mental states were accompanied by vibrations. You combine with what you vibrate to, so let us all now vibrate to success, happiness and abundance.

> Now is the appointed time. Today is the day of
> my amazing good fortune.

THE FORK IN THE ROAD

"Choose you this day whom ye will serve."—Josh. 24:15

Every day there is a necessity of choice (a fork in the road).

"Shall I do this, or shall I do that? Shall I go, or shall I stay?" Many people do not know what to do. They rush about letting other people make decisions for them, then regret having taken their advice.

There are others who carefully reason things out. They weigh and measure the situation like dealing in groceries, and are surprised when they fail to attain their goal.

There are still other people who follow the magic path of intuition and find themselves in their Promised Land in the twinkling of an eye.

Intuition is a spiritual faculty high above the reasoning mind, but on that path is all that you desire or require.

In my book "The Game of Life and How to Play It," I give many examples of success attained through using this marvelous faculty. I say also that prayer is telephoning to God and intuition is God telephoning to you. (Correspondence Course.)

So choose ye this day to follow the magic path of intuition.

In my question and answer classes I tell you how to cultivate intuition.

In most people it is a faculty which has remained dormant. So we say, "Awake thou that sleepeth. Wake up to your leads and hunches. Wake up to the divinity within!"

Claude Bragdon said, "To live intuitively is to live fourth dimensionally."

Now it is necessary for you to make a decision, you face a fork in the road. *Ask for a definite unmistakable lead,* and you will receive it.

We find many events to interpret metaphysically in the Book of Joshua. "After the death of Moses, the divine command came to Joshua, 'Now therefore, arise, go over the Jordan, thou and all thy people, unto the land which I do give to them. Every place the sole of your feet shall tread upon; to you have I given it'."

The feet are the symbol of understanding, so it means metaphysically all that we understand stands under us in consciousness, and what is rooted there can never be taken from us.

For, the bible goes on to say: "There shall not any man be able to stand before thee all the days of thy life...I will not fail thee, nor forsake thee. Only be thou strong and very courageous, that thou mayest observe to do according to all the law, which Moses my servant commanded thee: turn not from it to the right hand or to the left, that thou mayest prosper whithersoever thou goest."

So we find we have success through being strong and very courageous in following spiritual law. We are back again to the "fork in the road"—the necessity of choice.

"Choose you this day whom ye will serve," the intellect or divine guidance.

A well-known man, who has become a great power in the financial world, said to a friend, "I always follow intuition and I am luck incarnate."

Inspiration (which is divine guidance) is the most important thing in life. People come to Truth meetings for inspiration. I find the right word will start divine activity operating in their affairs.

A woman came to me with a complication of affairs. I said to her, "Let God juggle the situation." It clicked. She took the affirmation, "I now let God juggle this situation." Almost immediately she rented a house, which had been vacant for a long time.

Let God juggle every situation, for when you try to juggle the situation, you drop all the balls.

In my question and answer classes, I would be asked, "How do you let God juggle a situation, and what do you mean when you say I should not juggle it?"

You juggle with the intellect. The intellect would say, "Times are hard, no activity in real estate. Don't expect anything until the Fall of 1958."

With spiritual law there is only the *now*. Before you call you are answered, for "time and space are but a dream," and *your blessing is there waiting for you to release it by faith and the word.*

"Choose you this day whom ye will serve," fear or faith.

In every act prompted by fear lies the germ of its own defeat.

It takes much strength and courage to trust God. We often trust him in little things, but when it comes to a big situation we feel we had better attend to it ourselves; then comes defeat and failure.

The following extract from a letter which I received from a woman in the West shows how conditions can change in the twinkling of an eye.

"I've had the pleasure of reading your wonderful book, 'The Game of Life and How to Play It.' I have four boys, ten, thirteen, fifteen and seventeen, and thought how wonderful for them to grasp it, in their early life, and be able to get things which are theirs by Divine Right.

"The lady who let me read her copy gave me other things to read, but it seemed when I picked this book up it was magnetic and I could not let go of it. After reading it I realized, I was trying to live Divinely but did not understand the law, or I would have been much further advanced.

"At first I thought it quite hard to find a place in the business world, after so many years of being a mother. But I got this statement, '*God makes a way where there is no way.*' And He did that very thing for me.

"I am grateful for my position, and smile when people say, 'How do you do it, manage four growing boys, a home, after all the times you have been hospitalized with such major operations, and none of your relatives near you?'"

I have that statement in my book, "*God makes a way where there is no way.*"

God made a way for her in business when all her friends said it couldn't be done.

The average person will tell you almost anything can't be done.

I had an example of this the other day. In a shop I found a delightful little silver dripolator which would make just one cup of anything. I showed it to some friends with enthusiasm, thinking it so very cute, and one said, "It will never work." The other said, "If it belonged to me, I'd throw it away." I stood up for the little dripolator and said I knew it would work, which it did.

My friends were simply typical of the average person who says, "It can't be done."

All big ideas meet with opposition.

Do not let other people rock your boat.

Follow the path of wisdom and understanding, "and turn not from it to the right hand or to the left, that thou mayest prosper whithersoever thou goest."

In the thirteenth verse of the twenty-fourth chapter of Joshua, we read a remarkable statement: "And I have given you a land for which ye did not labour, and cities which ye built not, and ye dwell in them; of the vineyards and oliveyards which ye planted not, do ye eat."

This shows that man cannot *earn* anything, his blessings come as gifts. (Gifts lest any man shall boast.)

With the *realization of wealth*, we receive the gift of wealth.

With the *realization of success*, we receive the gift of success, for success and abundance are states of mind.

"For it is the Lord our God, he it is, that brought us up, and our fathers out of the land of Egypt, out of the house of bondage."

The land of Egypt stands for darkness—the house of bondage, where man is a slave to his doubts and fears, and beliefs in lack and limitation, the result of having followed the wrong fork in the road.

Misfortune is due to failure to stick to the things which spirit has revealed through intuition.

All big things have been accomplished by men who stuck to their big ideas.

Henry Ford was past middle age when the idea of the Ford car came to him. He had great difficulty in raising the money. His friends thought it was a crazy idea. His father said to him, tearfully, "Henry, why do you give up a good twenty-five dollar a week job in order to chase a crazy idea?" But no one could rock Henry Ford's boat.

So in order to come out of the land of Egypt, out of the house of bondage, we must make the right decisions.

Follow the right fork in the road. "Only be thou strong and very courageous, that thou mayest observe to do according to the law, which Moses my servant commanded thee: turn not from it to the right hand nor to the left, that thou mayest prosper whithersoever thou goest."

So, as we reach the fork in the road today, let us fearlessly follow the voice of intuition.

The bible calls it "the still small voice."

"There came a voice behind me, saying, 'This is the way, walk ye in it.'"

On this path is the good, already prepared for you.

You will find the "land for which ye did not labour, and cities which ye built not, and ye dwell in them; of the vineyards and oliveyards which ye planted not, do ye eat."

> I am divinely led, I follow the right fork in the road. God makes a way where there is no way.

XVII

CROSSING YOUR RED SEA

"Speak unto the children of Israel that they go forward."
—Ex. 14:15

One of the most dramatic stories in the bible is the episode of the children of Israel crossing the Red Sea.

Moses was leading them out of the land of Egypt where they were kept in bondage and slavery. They were being pursued by the Egyptians.

The children of Israel, like most people, did not enjoy trusting God; they did a lot of murmuring. They said to Moses: "Is not this the word that we did tell thee in Egypt, saying, Let us alone, that we may serve the Egyptians? For it had been better for us to serve the Egyptians, than that we should die in the wilderness."

And Moses said unto the people, "Fear ye not, stand still, and see the salvation of the Lord, which he will show to you today: for the Egyptians whom ye have seen today, ye shall see them again no more for ever."

"The Lord shall fight for you, and ye shall hold your peace."

We might say that Moses pounded faith into the children of Israel.

They preferred being slaves to their old doubts and fears (for Egypt stands for darkness), than to take the giant swing into faith, and pass through the wilderness to their Promised Land.

There is, indeed, a wilderness to pass through before your Promised Land is reached.

The old doubts and fears encamp round about you, but, there is always someone to tell you to go forward! There is always a Moses on your pathway. Sometimes it is a friend, sometimes intuition!

"And the Lord said to Moses, Wherefore criest thou unto me? Speak unto the children of Israel, that *they go forward!*"

"But lift thou up thy rod, and stretch out thine hand over the sea, and divide it: and the children of Israel shall go on dry ground through the midst of the sea."

"And Moses stretched out his hand over the sea; and the Lord caused the sea to go back by a strong east wind all that night, and made the sea dry land, and the waters were divided."

"And the children of Israel went into the midst of the sea upon the dry ground: and the waters were a wall unto them on their right hand, and on their left."

"And the Egyptians pursued, and went in after them to the midst of the sea, even all Pharaoh's horses, his chariots, and his horsemen."

"And the Lord said unto Moses, Stretch out thine hand over the sea, that the waters may come again upon the Egyptians, upon their chariots, and upon their horsemen."

"And Moses stretched forth his hand over the sea, and the sea returned; and the Egyptians fled against it; and the Lord overthrew the Egyptians in the midst of the sea."

CHAPTER XVII

"And the waters returned, and covered the chariots, and the horsemen, and all the hosts of Pharaoh that came into the sea after them; there remained not so much as one of them."

Now remember, the bible is talking about the individual. It is talking about your wilderness, your Red Sea, and *your* Promised Land.

Each one of you has a Promised Land, a heart's desire, but you have been so enslaved by the Egyptians (your negative thoughts), it seems very far away, and too good to be true. You consider trusting God a very risky proposition. The wilderness might prove worse than the Egyptians.

And how do you know your Promised Land really exists?

The reasoning mind will always back up the Egyptians.

But sooner or later, something says, "*Go forward!*" It is usually circumstances—you are driven to it.

I give the example of a student.

She is a very marvelous pianist and had great success abroad. She came back with a book full of press clippings, and a happy heart.

A relative took an interest in her and said she would back her financially for a concert tour. They chose a manager who took charge of the expenses, and attended to her bookings.

After a concert or two, there were no more funds. The manager had taken them. My friend was left stranded, desolate and disappointed. This was about the time that she came to me.

She hated the man, and it was making her ill. She had very little money and could afford only a cheerless room where her hands were often too cold to practice.

She was indeed, in bondage to the Egyptians—hate, resentment, lack and limitation.

Someone brought her to one of my meetings, and she spoke to me and told her story.

I said, "In the first place you must stop hating that man. When you are able to forgive him, your success will come back to you. You are taking your initiation in forgiveness."

It seemed a pretty big order, but she tried and came regularly to all my meetings.

In the meantime, the relative had started a suit to recover the money. Time went on and it never came to court.

My friend had a call to go to California. She was no longer disturbed by the situation, and had forgiven the man.

Suddenly, after about four years, she was notified that the case had come to court. She called me upon her arrival in New York, and asked me to speak the word for rightness and justice.

They went at the time appointed, and it was all settled out of court, the man restoring the money by monthly payments.

She came to me overflowing with joy, for she said, "I hadn't the least resentment toward the man. He was amazed when I greeted him cordially." Her relative said that all the money was to go to her, so she found herself with a big bank account.

Now she will soon reach her Promised Land. She came out of the house of bondage (of hate and resentment) and crossed her red sea. Her goodwill toward the man caused the waters to part, and she crossed over on dry land.

Dry land symbolizes something substantial under your feet, the feet symbolizing understanding.

Moses stands out as one of the greatest figures in biblical history.

CHAPTER XVII

"It came to Moses to move from Egypt with his nation. The task before him was not only the unwillingness of Pharaoh to let go of those whom he had made into profitable slaves, but also to stimulate to open rebellion this nation which had lost its initiative under the hardships of its taskmasters."

"It required extraordinary genius to meet this condition, which Moses possessed with self abnegation and the courage of his own convictions. Self abnegation! He was called the meekest of men. We have often heard the expression, 'As meek as Moses.' He was so meek towards the commands of the Lord, that he became one of the strongest of men."

The Lord said to Moses, "lift thou up thy rod, and stretch out thine hand over the sea, and divide it: and the children of Israel shall go on dry ground through the midst of the sea."

So, never doubting, he said to the children of Israel, "Go forward." This was a daring thing to do, to lead a multitude of people into the sea, having perfect faith they would not drown.

Behold the miracle!

"...the Lord caused the sea to go back by a strong east wind all that night, and made the sea dry land, and the waters were divided."

Now remember, this could happen *for you* this very day. Think of your problem.

Maybe you have lost your initiative from living so long a slave to Pharaoh—(your doubts, fears and discouragements).

Say to yourself, "*Go forward.*"

"...the Lord caused the sea to go back by a strong east wind."

We will think of this strong east wind as a strong affirmation.

Take a vital statement of Truth. For example, if your problem is a financial one, say: "*My supply comes from God, and big happy financial surprises now come to me, under grace, in perfect ways.*" The statement is a good one, for it contains the element of mystery.

We are told that God works in mysterious ways His wonders to perform. We might say in surprising ways. Now that you have made your statement for supply, you have caused the east wind to blow.

So walk up to your Red Sea of lack or limitation. The way to walk up to your Red Sea is to do something to show your fearlessness.

I will tell the story of a student who had an invitation to visit friends at a very fashionable summer resort.

She had been living in the country for a long time, grown heavier, and nothing fitted her but her girl scout suit. Suddenly, she received the invitation. It meant evening clothes, slippers and accessories, none of which she had, and no money to buy them. She came to me. I said, "What is your hunch?"

She replied, "I feel very fearless. I have the hunch to go, anyway."

So she squeezed herself into something to travel in, and went.

When she arrived at her friend's house she was greeted warmly, but her hostess said, with some embarrassment, "Maybe what I've done will hurt you, but there are some evening clothes and slippers I never wear which I have put in your room. Won't you make use of them?"

My friend assured her she would be delighted—and everything fitted perfectly.

Chapter XVII

She had, indeed, walked up to her Red Sea and passed over on dry land.

> The waters of my Red Sea part, and I pass over on dry land, I now go forward into my Promised Land.

THE WATCHMAN AT THE GATE

"Also I set watchmen over you, saying, Hearken to the sound of the trumpet."—Jeremiah 6:17

We must all have a watchman at the gate of our thoughts. The Watchman at the Gate is the superconscious mind.

We have the power to choose our thoughts.

Since we have lived in the race thought for thousands of years, it seems almost impossible to control them. They rush through our minds like stampeding cattle or sheep.

But a single sheep-dog can control the frightened sheep and guide them into the sheep pen.

I saw a picture in the news-reels of a shepherd-dog controlling the sheep. He had rounded up all but three. These three resisted and resented. They baahed and lifted their front feet in protest, but the dog simply sat down in front and never took his eyes off them. He did not bark or threaten. He just sat and looked his determination. In a little while the sheep tossed their heads and went in the pen.

We can learn to control our thoughts in the same way, by gentle determination, not force.

We take an affirmation and repeat it continually, while our thoughts are on the rampage.

We cannot always control our thoughts, but we *can control our words*, and repetition impresses the subconscious, and we are then master of the situation.

In the sixth chapter of Jeremiah we read: "I set a watchman over you, saying, Hearken to the sound of the trumpet."

Your success and happiness in life depend upon the watchman at the gate of your thoughts, for your thoughts, sooner or later, crystallize on the external.

People think by running away from a negative situation, they will be rid of it, but the same situation confronts them wherever they go.

They will meet the same experiences until they have learned their lessons. This idea is brought out in the moving picture, "The Wizard of Oz."

The little girl, Dorothy, is very unhappy because the mean woman in the village wants to take away her dog, Toto.

She goes, in despair, to confide in her Aunt Em and Uncle Henry, but they are too busy to listen, and tell her to "run along."

She says to Toto, "There is somewhere, a wonderful place high above the skies where everybody is happy and no one is mean." How she would love to be there!

A Kansas cyclone suddenly comes along, and she and Toto are lifted up, high in the sky, and land in the country of Oz.

Everything seems very delightful at first, but soon she has the same old experiences. The mean old woman of the village has turned into a terrible witch, and is still trying to get Toto from her.

CHAPTER XVIII

How she wishes she were back in Kansas.

She is told to find the Wizard of Oz. He is all powerful and will grant her request.

She starts off to find his palace in the Emerald City.

On the way she meets a scarecrow. He is so unhappy because he hasn't a brain.

She meets a man made of tin, who is so unhappy because he hasn't a heart.

Then she meets a lion who is so unhappy because he has no courage.

She cheers them up by saying, "We'll all go to the Wizard of Oz and he'll give us what we want"—the scarecrow a brain, the tin man a heart, and the lion courage.

They encounter terrible experiences, for the bad witch is determined to capture Dorothy and take away Toto and the ruby slippers which protect her.

At last they reach the Emerald Palace of the Wizard of Oz.

They ask for an audience, but are told no one has ever seen the Wizard of Oz, who lives mysteriously in the palace.

But through the influence of the good witch of the North, they enter the palace. There they discover that the Wizard is just a fake magician from Dorothy's home town in Kansas.

They are all in despair because their wishes cannot be granted!

But then the good witch shows them that their wishes are *already* granted. The scarecrow has developed a brain by having to decide what to do in the experiences he has encountered, the tin man finds he has a heart because he loves Dorothy, and the lion has become courageous because he *had* to show courage in his many adventures.

The good witch from the North says to Dorothy, "What have you learned from your experiences?" and Dorothy replies, "I have learned that my heart's desire is in my own home and in my own front yard." So the good witch waves her wand, and Dorothy is at home again.

She wakes up and finds that the scarecrow, the tin man, and the lion are the men who work on her uncle's farm. They are so glad to have her back. This story teaches *that if you run away your problems will run after you.*

Be *undisturbed* by a situation, and it will fall away of its own weight.

There is an occult law of indifference. "None of these things moves me." "None of these things disturbs me;" we might say in modern language.

When you can no longer be disturbed, all disturbance will disappear from the external.

"When your eyes have seen your teachers, your teachers disappear."

"I set watchmen over you, saying, Hearken to the sound of the trumpet."

A trumpet is a musical instrument, used in olden times, to draw people's attention to something; to victory, to order.

You will form the habit of giving attention to every thought and word, when you realize their importance.

The imagination, the scissors of the mind, is constantly cutting out the events to come into your life.

Many people are cutting out fear-pictures. Seeing things which are not divinely planned.

CHAPTER XVIII

With the "single eye," man sees only the Truth. He sees through evil, knowing that out of it comes good. He transmutes injustice into justice, and disarms his seeming enemy by sending *goodwill.*

We read in mythology of the Cyclops, a race of giants, said to have inhabited Sicily. These giants had only one eye in the middle of the forehead.

The seat of the imagining faculty is situated in the forehead (between the eyes). So these fabled giants came from this idea.

You are indeed a giant when you have a single eye. Then every thought will be a constructive thought, and every word, a word of Power.

Let the third eye be the watchman at the gate.

"If therefore thine eye be single, thy whole body is full of light."

With the single eye your body will be transformed into your spiritual body, the "body electric" made in God's likeness and image (imagination).

By seeing clearly the perfect plan, we could redeem the world: with our *inner eye* seeing a world of peace and plenty and good will.

"Judge not by appearances, judge righteous judgment."

"Nation shall not lift up sword against nation, neither shall they learn war anymore."

The occult law of indifference means that you are undisturbed by adverse appearances. You hold steadily to the *constructive thought,* which *wins out.*

Spiritual law transcends the law of Karma.

This is the attitude of mind which must be held by the healer or practitioner towards his patient.

Indifferent to appearances of lack, loss or sickness, he brings about the change in mind, body and affairs.

Let me quote from the thirty-first chapter of Jeremiah. The keynote is one of rejoicing. It gives a picture of the individual freed from negative thinking.

"For there shall be a day that the watchmen upon the mount Ephraim shall cry, Arise ye, and let us go up to Zion unto the Lord our God."

The Watchman at the Gate neither slumbers nor sleeps. It is the "eye which watches over Israel."

But the individual, living in a world of negative thought, is not conscious of this inner eye.

He may occasionally have flashes of intuition or illumination, then falls back into a world of chaos.

It takes determination and eternal vigilance to check up on words and thoughts. Thoughts of fear, failure, resentment and ill-will must be dissolved and dissipated.

Take the statement: "Every plant my father in heaven has not planted shall be rooted up."

This gives you a vivid picture of rooting up weeds in a garden. They are thrown aside, and dry up because they are without soil to nourish them.

You nourish negative thoughts by giving them your attention. Use the occult law of indifference and refuse to be interested.

Soon you will starve out the "army of the aliens." Divine ideas will crowd your consciousness, false ideas fade away, and you will desire only that which God desires through you.

CHAPTER XVIII

The Chinese have a proverb, "The Philosopher leaves the cut of his coat to the tailor."

So leave the plan of your life to the Divine Designer, and you will find all conditions permanently perfect.

The ground I am on is holy ground. I now expand rapidly into the divine plan of my life, where all conditions are permanently perfect.

THE WAY OF ABUNDANCE

"Then shalt thou lay up gold as dust."—Job 22:24

The way of abundance is a one-way street.

As the old saying is, "there are no two ways about it."

You are either heading for lack, or heading for abundance. The man with a rich consciousness and the man with a poor consciousness are not walking on the same mental street.

There is a lavish supply, divinely planned for each individual.

The rich man is tapping it, for rich thoughts produce rich surroundings.

Change your thoughts, and in the twinkling of an eye, all your conditions change. Your world is a world of crystallized ideas, crystallized words.

Sooner or later, you reap the fruits of your words and thoughts.

"Words are bodies or forces which move spirally and return in due season to cross the lives of their creators." People who are always talking lack and limitation, reap lack and limitation.

You cannot enter the Kingdom of Abundance bemoaning your lot.

I know a woman who had always been limited in her ideas of prosperity. She was continually making her old clothes "do," instead of buying new clothes. She was very careful of what money she had, and was always advising her husband not to spend so much. She said repeatedly, "I don't want anything I can't afford."

She couldn't afford much, so she didn't have much. Suddenly her whole world cracked up. Her husband left her, weary of her nagging and limited thoughts. She was in despair, when one day she came across a book on metaphysics. It explained the power of thought and words.

She realized that she had invited every unhappy experience by wrong thinking. She laughed heartily at her mistakes, and decided to profit by them. She determined *to prove the law of abundance.*

She used what money she had, fearlessly, to show her faith in her invisible supply. She relied upon God as the source of her prosperity. She no longer voiced lack and limitation. She kept herself feeling and looking prosperous.

Her old friends scarcely recognized her. She had swung into the way of abundance. More money came to her than she had ever had before. Unheard-of doors opened—amazing channels were freed. She became very successful in a work she had had no training for.

She found herself on *miracle ground.* What had happened?

She had changed the quality of her words and thoughts. She had taken God into her confidence, and into all her affairs. She had many eleventh-hour demonstrations, but her supply always came, for she dug her ditches and gave thanks without wavering.

Someone called me up recently and said, "I am looking desperately for a position."

I replied, "Don't look desperately for it, look for it with praise and thanksgiving, for Jesus Christ, the greatest of metaphysicians, said to pray with praise and thanksgiving."

Praise and thanksgiving open the gates, for expectancy always wins.

Of course, the law is impersonal, and a dishonest person with rich thoughts will attract riches—but, "a thing ill-got has ever bad success," as Shakespeare says. It will be of short duration and will not bring happiness.

We have only to read the papers to see that the way of the transgressor is hard.

That is the reason it is so necessary to make your demands aright on the Universal Supply, and ask for what is yours by divine right and under grace in a perfect way.

Some people attract prosperity, but cannot hold it. Sometimes their heads are turned, sometimes they lose it through fear and worry.

A friend in one of my question and answer classes told this story.

Some people in his home town, who had always been poor, suddenly struck oil in their back yard. It brought great riches. The father joined the country club and went in for golf. He was no longer young—the exercise was too much for him and he dropped dead on the links.

This filled the whole family with fear. They all decided they might have heart trouble, so they are now in bed with trained nurses watching every heart beat.

In the race-thought people must worry about something.

They no longer worried about money, so they shifted their worries to health.

The old idea was, "that you can't have everything." If you got one thing, you'd lose another. People were always saying, "Your luck won't last," "It's too good to be true."

Jesus Christ said, "In the world (world thought) there is tribulation, but be of good cheer, I have overcome the world (thought)."

In the superconscious (or Christ within), there is a lavish supply for every demand, and your good is perfect and permanent.

"If thou return to the Almighty, thou shalt be built up (in consciousness), thou shalt put away iniquity far from thy tabernacles."

"Then shalt thou lay up gold as dust, the gold of Ophir as the stones of the brooks."

"Yea, the Almighty shall be thy defense and thou shalt have plenty of silver."

What a picture of opulence! The result of "Returning to the Almighty (in consciousness)."

With the average person (who has thought in terms of lack for a long time) it is very difficult to build up a rich consciousness.

I have a student who has attracted great success by making the statement: "*I am the daughter of the King! My rich Father now pours out his abundance upon me: I am the daughter of the King! Everything makes way for me.*"

Many people put up with limited conditions because they are too lazy (mentally), to think themselves out of them.

You must have a great desire for financial freedom, you must feel yourself rich, you must see yourself rich, you must continually prepare for riches. Become as a little child and make believe you are rich. You are then impressing the subconscious with expectancy.

The imagination is man's workshop, the scissors of the mind, where he is constantly cutting out the events of his life!

The superconscious is the realm of inspiration, revelation, illumination and intuition.

Intuition is usually known as a hunch. I do not apologize for the word "hunch" anymore. It is now in Webster's latest dictionary.

I had a hunch to look up "hunch," and there it was.

The superconscious is the realm of perfect ideas. The great genius captures his thoughts from the superconscious.

"Without the vision (imagination) my people perish."

When people have lost the power to image their good, they "perish" (or go under).

It is interesting to compare the translation of the French and English Bibles. In the 21st verse of the 22nd chapter of Job we read: "Acquaint now thyself with him, and be at peace: thereby good shall come unto thee." In the French Bible we read: "Attach thyself to God and you will have peace. Thou shalt thus enjoy happiness."

The 23rd verse: "If thou return to the Almighty, thou shalt be built up, thou shalt put away iniquity far from thy tabernacles." In the French translation we read: "Thou shalt be re-established if thou returnest to the Almighty, putting iniquity far off from your dwellings."

In the 24th verse we read a new and amazing translation. The English Bible reads: "Then shalt thou lay up gold as dust, and the gold of Ophir as the stones of the brooks." The French Bible says: "Throw gold into the dust, the gold of Ophir amongst the pebbles of the torrents; and the Almighty shall be thy gold, thy silver, thy riches."

This means if people are depending entirely on their visible supply, it is even better to throw it away and trust absolutely to the Almighty for gold, silver and riches.

I give an example in the story told me by a friend.

A priest went to visit a nunnery in France, where they fed many children. One of the nuns, in despair, told the priest they had no food; the children must go hungry. She said that they had but one piece of silver (about the value of a quarter of a dollar). They needed food and clothing.

The priest said, "Give me the coin."

She handed it to him and he threw it out the window.

"Now," he said, "rely entirely upon God." Within a short time friends arrived with plenty of food and gifts of money.

This does not mean to throw away what money you have, but don't depend upon it. Depend upon your invisible supply, the Bank of the Imagination.

Let us now attach ourselves to God and have peace. For He shall be our gold, our silver and our riches.

> The inspiration of the Almighty shall be my
> defense and I shall have plenty of silver.

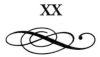

I SHALL NEVER WANT

"The Lord is my Shepherd; I shall not want."—Psalms 23:1

The 23rd Psalm is the best known of all the Psalms—we might say that it is the keynote to the message of the Bible.

It tells man he shall never want, when he has the realization (or conviction) that the Lord is his Shepherd: the *realization* that Infinite Intelligence supplies every need.

If you get this conviction today, every need will be met now and forever-more; you will draw, instantly, from the abundance of the spheres, whatever you desire or require; for what you need is *already on your pathway.*

A woman suddenly had the realization: "The Lord is my Shepherd, I shall never want." She seemed to be touching her invisible supply, she felt outside of Time and Space, she no longer relied on the external.

Her first demonstration was a small, but necessary one. She needed at once, some large paperclips, but had no time to go to a stationer's to buy them.

In looking for something else, she opened a little-used chest, and in it, she found about a dozen large paperclips.

She felt that the law was working, and gave thanks; then some needed money appeared, things large and small came her way.

Since then she has relied upon the statement: "The Lord is my Shepherd, I shall never want."

We used to hear people say, "I do not think it is right to ask God for money or things."

They did not realize that this Creative Principle is within each man.—(The Father within). True Spirituality is proving God as your supply, daily—not just once in a while.

Jesus Christ knew this law, for whatever He desired or required, appeared immediately on His pathway, the loaves and fishes and money from the fish's mouth.

With this realization, all hoarding and saving would disappear.

This does not mean that you should not have a big bank account, and investments, but it does mean that you should not depend upon them, for if you had a loss in one direction, you would have a gain in another.

Always "your barns would be full and your cup flow over."

Now, how does one make this contact with his invisible supply? By taking a statement of Truth which clicks and gives him realization.

This is not open to a chosen few, "Whosoever calleth on the name of the Lord shall be delivered." The Lord is *your* shepherd and *my* shepherd and everybody's shepherd.

God is the Supreme Intelligence devoted to supplying man's need; the explanation is, that man is God in action. Jesus Christ said, "I and the Father are one."

We might paraphrase the statement and say, I and the great Creative Principle of the Universe, are one and the same.

Man only lacks when he loses his contact with this Creative Principle, which must be fully trusted, for it is Pure Intelligence and knows the way of Fulfillment.

The reasoning mind and personal will, cause a short circuit.

"Trust in me and I will bring it to pass."

Most people are filled with apprehension and dread, when there is nothing to cling to on the external.

A woman came to a practitioner and said, "I'm only a poor little woman with no one but God back of me." The practitioner said,—"You need not worry if you have God back of you," for "all that the Kingdom affords is yours."

A woman called me on the phone and said, almost in tears, "I'm so worried about the business situation." I replied, "The situation with God remains the same: The Lord is your Shepherd: you shall not want." "If one door shuts, another door opens."

A very successful business-man who conducts all affairs on Truth methods, said, "The trouble with most people is, that they get to relying on certain conditions. They haven't enough imagination to go forward—to open new channels."

Nearly every big success is built upon a failure.

I was told that Edgar Bergen lost his part in a Broadway production because they did not want any more dummies. Noel Coward got him on the Rudy Vallee radio hour, and he and Charlie McCarthy became famous overnight.

I told the story, at one of my meetings, of a man who was so poor and discouraged, that he ended it all. A few days later, came a letter notifying him that he had inherited a large fortune.

A man in the meeting said: "That means, when you want to be dead, your demonstration is three days off." Yes, *do not be fooled by the darkness before the dawn.*

It is a good thing to see the dawn once in a while, to convince you how unfailing it is. It reminds me of an experience of several years ago.

I had a friend who lived in Brooklyn near Prospect Park. She liked to do unusual things and said to me: "Come to visit me and we'll get up early and see the sun-rise in Prospect Park."

At first I refused, and then came the hunch that it would be an interesting experience.

It was in the summer. We got up about four o'clock,—my friend, her little daughter and myself. It was pitch dark, but we sallied forth down the street, to the entrance of the Park.

Some policemen eyed us curiously, but my friend said to them with dignity, "We are going to see the sun-rise" and it seemed to satisfy them. We walked through the Park to the beautiful rose-garden.

A faint pink streak appeared in the East, then suddenly, we heard a most tremendous uproar. We were near the Zoo and all the animals were greeting the dawn.

The lions and tigers roared, the hyenas laughed, there were shrieks and howls: every animal had something to say, for a new day was at hand.

It was indeed, most inspiring. The light slanted through the trees; everything had an unearthly aspect.

Then, as it grew lighter, our shadows were in front instead of behind us. The dawn of a new day!

This is the wonderful dawn which comes to each one of us, after some darkness.

Your dawn of Success, Happiness and Abundance is sure to come.

Every day is important, for we read in the wonderful Sanskrit poem, "Look well, therefore, to this day, such is the salutation of the dawn."

This day the Lord is your Shepherd! This day, you shall not want; as you and this great Creative Principle are one and the same.

The 34th Psalm is also a Psalm of security. It starts with a blessing for the Lord, "I will bless the Lord at all times: His praise shall continually be in my mouth."

"They that seek the Lord shall not want any good thing." Seeking the Lord means that man must make the first move. "Draw near to me and I will draw near to thee, saith the Lord."

You seek the Lord by making your affirmation, expecting and preparing for your good.

If you ask for success and prepare for failure, you will receive the thing you have prepared for.

I tell in my book, "The Game of Life and How to Play It," of a man who asked me to speak the word that all his debts be wiped out.

After the treatment, he said, "Now I'm thinking what I'll say to the people when I haven't the money to pay them." A treatment won't help you if you haven't faith in it, for faith and expectancy impress the subconscious mind with the picture of fulfillment.

In the 23rd Psalm we read, "He restoreth my soul." Your soul is your subconscious mind and must be restored with the right ideas.

Whatever you feel deeply is impressed upon the subconscious, and manifests in your affairs.

If you are convinced that you are a failure, you will be a failure, until you impress the subconscious with the conviction you are a success.

This is done by making an affirmation which "clicks."

A friend in a meeting said that I had given her the statement as she was leaving the room—"*The ground you are on is harvest ground.*" Things with her, had been very dull; but this statement clicked.

"*Harvest Ground, Harvest Ground,*" rang in her ears. Good things immediately commenced to come to her, and happy surprises.

The reason it is necessary to make an affirmation is because repetition impresses the subconscious. You cannot control your thoughts at first, but you can control your words, and Jesus Christ said: "By your *words* you are justified and by your words you are condemned."

Every day, choose the right words; the right thoughts!

The Imaging faculty is the creative faculty: "Out of the imaginations of the heart come the issues of life."

We have all a bank we can draw upon, the Bank of the Imagination.

Let us imagine ourselves rich, well and happy: imagine all our affairs in divine order; but leave the way of fulfillment to Infinite Intelligence.

CHAPTER XX

"He has weapons ye know not of," He has channels which will surprise you.

One of the most important passages in the 23rd Psalm is— "Thou preparest a table before me in the presence of mine enemies."

This means that even in the presence of the enemy situation, brought on by your doubts, fears or resentments, a way out is prepared for you.

The Lord is my Shepherd; I shall never want.

LOOK WITH WONDER

"I will remember the works of the Lord; surely I will remember thy wonders of old."—Psalms 77:11

The words wonder and wonderful are used many times in the Bible. In the dictionary the word wonder is defined as, "a cause for surprise, astonishment, a miracle, a marvel."

Ouspensky, in his book, "Tertium Organum," calls the 4th dimensional world, the "World of the Wondrous." He has figured out mathematically, that there is a realm where all conditions are perfect. Jesus Christ called it the Kingdom.

We might say, "Seek ye first the world of the wondrous, and all things shall be added unto you."

It can only be reached through a state of consciousness.

Jesus Christ said, to enter the Kingdom, we must become "as a little child." Children are continually in a state of joy and wonder!

The future holds promises of mysterious good. Anything can happen over night.

Robert Louis Stevenson, in "A Child's Garden of Verses" says: "The world is so full of a number of things, I'm sure we should all be as happy as kings."

So let us look with wonder at that which is before us; that statement was given me a number of years ago, I mention it in my book, "The Game of Life and How to Play It."

I had missed an opportunity and felt that I should have been more awake to my good. The next day, I took the statement early in the morning, "I look with wonder at that which is before me."

At noon the phone rang, and the proposition was put to me again. This time I grasped it: I did indeed, look with wonder for I never expected the opportunity to come to me again.

A friend in one of my meetings said the other day, that this statement had brought her wonderful results. It fills the consciousness with happy expectancy.

Children are filled with happy expectancy until grown-up people, and unhappy experiences bring them out of the world of the wondrous!

Let us look back and remember some of the gloomy ideas which were given us: "Eat the speckled apples first." "Don't expect too much, then you won't be disappointed." "You can't have everything in this life." "Childhood is your happiest time." "No one knows what the future will bring." What a start in life!

These are some of the impressions I picked up in early childhood.

At the age of six I had a great sense of responsibility. Instead of looking with wonder at that which was before me, I looked with fear and suspicion. I feel much younger now than I did when I was six.

I have an early photograph taken about that time, grasping a flower, but with a careworn and hopeless expression.

CHAPTER XXI

I had left the world of the wondrous behind me! I was now living in the world of realities, as my elders told me, and it was far from wondrous.

It is a great privilege for children to live in this age, when they are taught Truth from their birth. Even if they are not taught actual metaphysics, the ethers are filled with joyous expectancy.

You may become a Shirley Temple or a Freddy Bartholomew or a great pianist at the age of six, and go on a concert tour.

We are all now, back in the world of the wondrous, where anything can happen overnight, for when miracles do come, they come quickly!

So let us become *Miracle Conscious:* prepare for miracles, expect miracles, and we are then inviting them into our lives.

Maybe you need a financial miracle! There is a supply for every demand. Through active faith, the word, and intuition, we release this invisible supply.

I will give an example: One of my students found herself almost without funds, she needed one thousand dollars, and she had had plenty of money at one time and beautiful possessions, but had nothing left but an ermine wrap. No fur dealer would give her much for it.

I spoke the word that it would be sold to the right person for the right price, or that the supply would come in some other way. It was necessary that the money manifest at once, it was no time to worry or reason.

She was on the street making her affirmations. It was a stormy day—She said to herself, "I'm going to show active faith in my invisible supply by taking a taxi cab:" it was a very strong hunch. As she got out of the taxi, at her destination, a woman stood waiting to get in.

It was an old friend: a very very kind friend. It was the first time in her life she had ever taken a taxi, but her Rolls Royce was out of commission that afternoon.

They talked, and my friend told her about the ermine wrap; "Why," her friend said, "I will give you a thousand dollars for it." And that afternoon she had the cheque.

God's ways are ingenious, His methods are sure.

A student wrote me the other day, that she was using that statement—*God's ways are ingenious, His methods are sure.* A series of unexpected contacts brought about a situation she had been desiring. She looked with wonder at the working of the law.

Our demonstrations usually come within a "split second." All is timed with amazing accuracy in Divine Mind.

My student left the taxi, just as her friend stopped to enter; a second later, she would have hailed another taxi.

Man's part is to be wide awake to his leads and hunches; for on the magic path of Intuition is all that he desires or requires.

In Moulton's Modern Reader's Bible, the book of Psalms is recognized as the perfection of lyric poetry.

"The musical meditation which is the essence of lyrics can find no higher field than the devout spirit which at once raises itself to the service of God, and overflows on the various sides of active and contemplative life."

The Psalms are also human documents, and I have selected the 77th Psalm because it gives the picture of a man in despair, but as he contemplates the wonders of God, faith and assurance are restored to him.

"I cried unto God with my voice, even unto God with my voice; and He gave ear unto me.

In the day of my trouble I sought the Lord: my soul refused to be comforted.

Will the Lord cast off forever? and will he be favourable no more?

Hath God forgotten to be gracious? hath he in anger shut up his tender mercies?

And I said, This is my infirmity: but I will remember the years of the right hand of the Most High.

I will remember the works of the Lord; surely I will remember thy wonders of old.

I will meditate also of all thy work, and talk of thy doings.

Thy way, O God, is in the sanctuary: who is so great a God as our God!

Thou art the God that doest wonders.

Thou hast with thine arm redeemed thy people."

This is a picture of what the average Truth student goes through, when confronted with a problem; he is assailed by thoughts of doubt, fear and despair.

Then some statement of Truth will flash into his consciousness—"God's ways are ingenious, His methods are sure!" He remembers other difficulties which have been overcome, his confidence in God returns. He thinks, *what God has done before, He will do for me and more!*

I was talking to a friend not long ago who said: "I would be pretty dumb if I didn't believe God could solve my problem. So many times before, wonderful things have come to me, I know they will come again!"

So the summing up of the 77th Psalm is, "What God has done before, He now does for me and more!"

It is a good thing to say when you think of your past success, happiness or wealth: all loss comes from your own vain imaginings, fear of loss crept into your consciousness, you carried burdens and fought battles, you reasoned instead of sticking to the magic path of intuition.

But in the twinkling of an eye, all will be restored to you—for as they say in the East—"What Allah has given, cannot be diminished."

Now to go back to the child's state of consciousness, you should be filled with wonder, but be careful not to live in your past childhood.

I know people who can only think about their happy childhood days: they remember what they wore! No skies have since been so blue, or grass so green. They therefore miss the opportunities of the wonderful now.

I will tell an amusing story of a friend who lived in a town when she was very young, then moved away to another city. She always looked back to the house they first lived in; to her it was an enchanted palace: large, spacious and glamorous.

Many years after, when she had grown up, she had an opportunity of visiting this house. She was disillusioned: she found it small, stuffy and ugly. Her idea of beauty had entirely changed, for in the front yard was an iron dog.

If you went back to your past, it would not be the same. So in this friend's family, they called living in the past, "iron-dogging."

Her sister told me a story of some "iron-dogging" she had done. When she was about sixteen, she met abroad, a very dashing and romantic young man, an artist. This romance didn't last long, but she talked about it a lot to the man she afterwards married.

Years rolled by, the dashing and romantic young man had become a well-known artist; and came to this country to have an exhibition of his pictures. My friend was filled with excitement, and hunted him up to renew their friendship. She went to his exhibition, and in walked a portly business man—no trace was left of the dashing romantic youth! When she told her husband, all he said was, "iron-dogging."

Remember, *now* is the appointed time! *Today* is the day! *And your good can happen overnight.*

Look with wonder at that which is before you!

We are filled with divine expectancy: "I will restore to you the years which the locusts have eaten!"

Now let each one think of the good which seems so difficult to attain; it may be health, wealth, happiness or perfect self-expression.

Do not think *how* your good can be accomplished, just give thanks that you have already received on the invisible plane, "therefore the steps leading up to it are secured also."

Be wide awake to your intuitive leads, and suddenly, you find yourself in your Promised Land.

I look with wonder at that which is before me.

XXII

CATCH UP WITH YOUR GOOD

"And it shall come to pass, that before they call, I will answer: and while they are yet speaking, I will hear."
—Isaiah 65:24

Catch up with your good! This is a new way of saying, "Before they call, I will answer."

Your good *precedes* you; it gets there before you do. But how to catch up with your good? For you must have ears that hear, and eyes that see, or it will escape you.

Some people never catch up with their good in life; they will say, "My life has always been one of hardship, no good luck ever comes to me." They are the people who have been asleep to their opportunities; or through laziness, haven't caught up with their good.

A woman told a group of friends that she had not eaten for three days. They dashed about asking people to give her work; but she refused it. She explained that she never got up until twelve o'clock, she liked to lie in bed and read magazines.

She just wanted people to support her while she read "Vogue" and "Harper's Bazaar." We must be careful not to slip into lazy states of mind. Take the affirmation, *I am wide awake to my good, I never miss a trick.* Most people are only half awake to their good.

A student said to me, "If I don't follow my hunches, I always get into a jam."

I will tell the story of a woman, one of my students, who followed her intuitive lead, which brought amazing results.

She had been asked to visit friends in a nearby town. She had very little money. When she arrived at her destination, she found the house locked up, they had gone away: she was filled with despair, then commenced to pray: she said, "Infinite Intelligence, give me a definite lead, let me know just what to do!"

The name of a certain hotel flashed into her consciousness—it persisted—the name seemed to stand out in big letters.

She had just enough money to get back to New York and the hotel. As she was about to enter, an old friend suddenly appeared, who greeted her warmly; and whom she hadn't seen for years.

She explained that she was living at the hotel but was going away for several months, and added, "Why don't you live in my suite while I am away:—it won't cost you a cent."

My friend accepted gratefully, and looked with amazement on the working of Spiritual law.

She had caught up with her good by following intuition.

All going forward comes from desire. Science today, is going back to Lamarck and his "dint—of wishing" theory. He claims that birds do not fly because they have wings, but they have wings because they wanted to fly; result of the "Push of the emotional wish."

Think of the irresistible power of thought with clear vision. Many people are in a fog most of the time, making wrong decisions and going the wrong way.

During the Christmas rush, my maid said to a saleswoman at one of the big shops, "I suppose this is your busiest day." She replied, "Oh no! the day *after* Christmas is our busiest day, when people bring most of the things back."

Hundreds of people choosing the wrong gifts because they were not listening to their intuitive leads.

No matter what you are doing, ask for guidance. It saves time and energy and often a lifetime of misery.

All suffering comes from the violation of intuition. Unless intuition builds the house, they labor in vain who build it.

Get the *habit of hunching*, then you will always be on the magic path.

"And it shall come to pass, that before they call, I will answer: and while they are yet speaking, I will hear."

Working with spiritual law, we are bringing to pass that which already is. In the Universal Mind it is there as an idea, but is crystallized on the external, by a sincere desire.

The idea of a bird was a perfect picture in divine mind; the fish caught the idea, and wished themselves into birds.

Are your desires bringing you wings? *We should all be bringing some seemingly impossible thing to pass.*

One of my affirmations is, "*The unexpected happens, my seemingly impossible good now comes to pass.*"

Do not magnify obstacles, magnify the Lord—that means, magnify God's power.

The average person will dwell on all the obstacles and hindrances which are there to prevent his good coming to pass.

You "combine with what you notice," so if you give obstacles and hindrances your undivided attention, they grow worse and worse.

Give God your undivided attention. Keep saying silently (in the face of all obstacles), *"God's ways are ingenious, His methods are sure."*

God's power is invincible, (though invisible). "Call unto me and I will answer thee, and show thee great and mighty things, which thou knowest not."

In demonstrating our good, we must look away from adverse appearances, "Judge not by appearances."

Get some statement which will give you a feeling of assurance, *The long arm of God reaches out over people and conditions, controlling the situation and protecting my interests!*

I was asked to speak the word for a man who was to have a business interview with a seemingly unscrupulous person. I used the statement, and rightness and justice came out of the situation, at just the exact time I was speaking.

We have all heard the quotation from Proverbs, "Hope deferred maketh the heart grow sick, but when the desire cometh, it is a tree of life."

In desiring sincerely (without anxiety), we are catching up with the thing desired; and the desire becomes crystallized on the external. "I will give to you the rightous desires of your heart."

Selfish desires, desires which harm others, always return to harm the sender.

The righteous desire might be called, an echo from the Infinite. It is already a perfect idea in divine mind.

All inventors catch up with the ideas of the articles they invent. I say in my book, "The Game of Life and How to Play It," the telephone was seeking Bell.

Chapter XXII

Often two people discover the same inventions at the same time; they have tuned in with the same idea.

The most important thing in life, is to bring the divine plan to pass.

Just as the picture of the oak is in the acorn, the divine design of your life is in your superconscious mind, and you must work out the perfect pattern in your affairs. You will then lead a magic life, for in the divine design, all conditions are permanently perfect.

People defy the divine design when they are asleep to their good.

Perhaps the woman who liked to lie in bed most of the day, and read magazines, should be writing for magazines, but her habits of laziness dulled all desire to go forward.

The fishes who desired wings, were alert and alive, they did not spend their days on the bed of the ocean, reading "Vogue" and "Harper's Bazaar."

Awake thou that sleepeth and catch up with your good!

"Call on me and I will answer thee, and show thee great and mighty things, which thou knowest not."

I now catch up with my good, for before I called
I was answered.

RIVERS IN THE DESERT

"Behold, I will do a new thing: now it shall spring forth; shall ye not know it? I will even make a way in the wilderness, and rivers in the desert."—Isaiah 43:19

In this 43rd chapter of Isaiah, are many wonderful statements, showing the irresistible power of Supreme Intelligence, coming to man's rescue in times of trouble. *No matter how impossible the situation seems, Infinite Intelligence knows the way out.*

Working with God-Power, man becomes unconditioned and absolute. Let us get a realization of this hidden power we can call upon at any moment.

Make your contact with Infinite Intelligence, (the God within) and all appearance of evil evaporates, for it comes from man's "vain imaginings."

In my question and answer class I would be asked, "How do you make a conscious contract with this Invincible Power?"

I reply, "By your word." "By your word you are justified."

The Centurion said to Jesus Christ, "Speak the word master and my servant shall be healed."

"Whosoever calleth on the name of the Lord shall be delivered." Notice the word, "call:" you are calling on the Lord or Law, when you make an affirmation of Truth.

As I always say, take a statement which "clicks," that means, gives you a feeling of security.

People are enslaved by ideas of lack; lack of love, lack of money, lack of companionship, lack of health, and so on.

They are enslaved by the ideas of interference and incompletion. They are asleep in the Adamic Dream: Adam (generic man,) ate of "Maya the tree of illusion" and saw two powers, good and evil.

The Christ mission was to wake people up to the Truth of one Power, God. "Awake thou that sleepeth."

If you lack any good thing, you are still asleep to your good.

How do you awake from the Adamic dream of opposites, after having slept soundly in the race thought for hundreds of years?

Jesus Christ said, "When two of you agree, it shall be done." It is the law of agreement.

It is almost impossible to see clearly, your good, for yourself: that is where the healer, practitioner or friend is necessary.

Many successful men say they have succeeded because their wives believed in them.

I will quote from a current newspaper, giving Walter P. Chrysler's tribute to his wife: "Nothing," he once said, "has given me more satisfaction in life, than the way my wife had faith in me from the very first, through all those years." Chrysler wrote of her, "It seemed to me I could not make any one understand that I was ambitious except Della. I could tell her and she would nod. It seems to me I even dared to tell her that I intended, some day, to be master mechanic." She always backed his ambitions.

CHAPTER XXIII

Talk about your affairs as little as possible, and then only to the ones who will give you encouragement and inspiration. The world is full of "Wet blankets," people who tell you "it can't be done," that you are aiming too high.

As people sit in Truth meetings and services, often a word or an idea will open a way in the wilderness.

Of course the Bible is speaking of states of consciousness. You are in a wilderness or desert, when you are out of harmony—when you are angry, resentful, fearful or undecided. Indecision is the cause of much ill health, being unable "to make up your mind."

One day when I was in a bus, a woman stopped it and asked the conductor its destination. He told her, but she was undecided. She got half way on, and then got off, then on again: the conductor turned to her and said, "Lady make up your mind!"

So it is with so many people: "Ladies make up your minds!"

The intuitive person is never undecided: he is given his leads and hunches, and goes boldly ahead, knowing he is on the magic path.

In Truth, we always ask for definite leads just what to do; you will always receive one if you ask for it. Sometimes it comes as intuition, sometimes from the external.

One of my students, named Ada, was walking down the street, undecided whether to go to a certain place, or not; she asked for a lead. Two women were walking in front of her. One turned to the other and said, "Why don't you go Ada?"— The woman's name just happened to be Ada—my friend took it as a definite lead, and went on to her destination, and the outcome was very successful.

We really lead magic lives, guided and provided for at every step; *if we have ears to hear and eyes that see.*

Of course we have left the plane of the intellect and are drawing from the superconscious, the God within, which says, "This is the way, walk ye in it."

Whatever you should know, will be revealed to you. Whatever you lack, will be provided! "Thus saith the Lord which maketh a way in the sea and a path in the mighty waters."

"Remember ye not the former things, neither consider the things of old."

People who live in the past have severed their contact with the wonderful now. God knows only the now; now is the appointed time, today is the day.

Many people lead lives of limitation, hoarding and saving, afraid to use what they have; which brings more lack and more limitation.

I give the example of a woman who lived in a small country town: she could scarcely see to get about, and had very little money. A kind friend took her to an oculist, and presented her with glasses, which enabled her to see perfectly. Sometime later she met her on the street without the glasses. She exclaimed, "Where are your glasses?"

The woman replied, "Well, you don't expect me to hack 'em out by using them every day, do you? I only wear them on Sundays."

You must live in the now and be wide awake to your opportunities.

"Behold, I will do a new thing: now it shall spring forth; shall ye not know it? I will even make a way in the wilderness, and rivers in the desert."

This message is meant for the individual: think of your problem and know that Infinite Intelligence knows the way of fulfillment. I say the *way*, for before you called you were answered. *The supply always precedes the demand.*

God is the Giver and the Gift and now creates His own amazing channels.

When you have asked for the Divine Plan of your life to manifest, you are protected from getting the things that are not in the Divine Plan.

You may think that all your happiness depends upon obtaining one particular thing in life; later on, you praise the Lord that you didn't get it.

Sometimes you are tempted to follow the reasoning mind, and argue with your intuitive leads, suddenly the Hand of Destiny pushes you into your right place; under grace, you find yourself back on the magic path again.

You are now wide awake to your good—you have the ears that hear (your intuitive leads,) and the eyes which see the open road of fulfillment.

The genius within me is released. I now fulfill my destiny.

THE INNER MEANING OF SNOW WHITE AND THE SEVEN DWARFS

I have been asked to give a Metaphysical interpretation of Snow White and the Seven Dwarfs, one of Grimm's Fairy Tales.

It is amazing how this picture, a fairy story, swept sophisticated New York, and the whole country, due to Walt Disney's genius.

This fairy tale was supposed to be for children, but men and women have packed the theatre. It is because fairy tales come down from old legends of Persia, India and Egypt, which are founded on Truth.

Snow White, the little Princess, has a cruel stepmother, who is jealous of her. This cruel stepmother idea appears also in "Cinderella."

Nearly everyone has a cruel step-mother. THE CRUEL STEP-MOTHER IS A NEGATIVE THOUGHT-FORM YOU HAVE BUILT UP IN THE SUBCONSCIOUS.

Snow White's cruel step-mother is jealous of her and always keeps her in rags and in the background.

ALL CRUEL THOUGHT FORMS DO THIS.

The cruel step-mother consults her magic mirror every day, saying: "Magic mirror on the wall, who is the fairest of them all?" One day the mirror replies: "Thou Queen, mayst fair and beauteous be, but Snow White is lovelier far than thee." This enrages the Queen, so she decides to send Snow White to the forest to be killed by one of her servants. However, the servant's heart melts when Snow White begs for her life, so he leaves her in the woods. The woods are filled with terrifying animals and many pitfalls and dangers. She falls in terror to the ground, and while there, a most unusual spectacle presents itself. Scores of the most delightful little animals and birds creep up and surround her. Rabbits, squirrels, deer, beavers, raccoons, etc. She opens her eyes and greets them with pleasure; they are so friendly and attractive. She tells her story and they lead her to a little house which she makes her home. NOW THESE FRIENDLY BIRDS AND ANIMALS SYMBOLIZE OUR INTUITIVE LEADS OR HUNCHES, WHICH ARE ALWAYS READY TO "GET YOU OUT OF THE WOODS."

The little house proves to be the home of the Seven Dwarfs. Everything is in disorder, so Snow White and her animal friends begin to clean the house. The squirrels dust with their tails, the birds hang things up, using the little deer's horns for a hat-rack. When the seven dwarfs come home from their work of digging gold, they discover the change and at last find Snow White asleep on one of the beds. In the morning she tells her story, remains with them to keep house and cook their meals, and is very happy. THE SEVEN DWARFS SYMBOLIZE THE PROTECTIVE FORCES ALL ABOUT US.

In the meantime, the cruel step-mother consults her mirror and it says to her: "Over the hills in the green wood shade, where the Seven Dwarfs their dwelling have made, there Snow White is hiding her head, and she, is lovelier far, Oh, Queen than thee." This infuriates the Queen; so she starts off disguised as an old hag, with a poisoned apple for Snow White. She finds her in the house of the Seven Dwarfs and tempts her with the big, red luscious apple. The birds and animals endeavor to tell her not to touch it. THEY TRY TO GIVE HER THE HUNCH NOT TO EAT IT. They rush around in dismay, but Snow White can't resist the apple, she takes one bite and falls, apparently dead. Now all the little birds and animals rush off to bring the Seven Dwarfs to the rescue; but too late, Snow White lies lifeless. They all bow their little heads in grief. Then suddenly the Prince appears, kisses Snow White, and she comes to life. They are married and live happily ever after. The Queen, the cruel stepmother, is swept away by a terrific storm, THE OLD THOUGHT-FORM IS DISSOLVED AND DISSIPATED FOREVER. THE PRINCE SYMBOLIZES THE DIVINE PLAN OF YOUR LIFE. WHEN IT WAKES YOU UP YOU LIVE HAPPILY EVER AFTER.

This is the fairy story which has enthralled New York and the whole country.

Find out what form of tyranny your cruel stepmother is taking in your subconscious. It is some negative conviction which works out in all your affairs.

We hear people saying: "My good always comes to me too late." "I've lost so many opportunities!" We must reverse the thought and say repeatedly: "*I am wide awake to my good, I never miss a trick.*"

WE MUST DROWN OUT THE DREARY SUGGESTIONS OF THE CRUEL STEPMOTHER. *ETERNAL VIGILANCE*

IS THE PRICE OF FREEDOM FROM THESE NEGATIVE THOUGHT-FORMS.

* * *

Nothing can hinder, nothing can delay the manifestation of the Divine Plan of my life.

The Light of Lights streams on my pathway, revealing the Open Road of Fulfillment!